Before God's Face
the Discipline of Coram Deo

by

Andy Daugherty

Each Voice Publishing

BEFORE GOD'S FACE
THE DISCIPLINE OF CORAM DEO

by

Andy Daugherty

Each Voice Publishing

$^{144}/_{5.18}$

Cover Design: Matthew Remion

Dedication

I dedicate this book to my mother, Jo Anne Daugherty, the person most responsible for introducing me to my Savior and modeling His love so excellently. You have my eternal gratitude.

Acknowledgments

In my life, I've been very blessed by many people. Some of these people were critical to the back-story of this book while others were integral to its actual production. I am very grateful for the love and support of my family: My wife Terri and my two children, Amy and Matthew. Without their love, this book would not have been possible.

I am also very thankful for my mother, for being the most loving parent anyone could ever ask for.

The Disciples class at McDonough Christian church has been a blessing to me for almost ten years. I wrote the core content of this study as handouts compiled into a workbook format starting in 2013. The class responded positively and several of the members encouraged me to seek a broader audience to bless others with this material. In late 2014, we formed a small team to enhance and edit the 40-page workbook into a 100-plus page manuscript that could be submitted to potential publishers.

Special thanks go to the proofing team: Alice Moore, Debbie Arnold, and Jim Irby. In addition, thanks to Dale Cramer for very valuable advice on writing.

Others I want to thank:
Scott Schade for encouraging me in many ways over the years,
John Leonard for referring me to Each Voice Publishing,
Paul Leslie for being the most caring pastor I've ever known and for writing the foreword,
The entire leadership and staff at McDonough Christian church for fostering such a Christ-centered church and for spurring me toward spiritual growth through discipleship,
And for Lisa Leonard, the editor-in-chief at Each Voice, for taking a chance on me and this manuscript.

BEFORE

GOD'S FACE

the discipline of Coram Deo

Brother Michael, O.S.L.
1Timothy 1:12
Saint-Luke.net
267-650-4720

Table of Contents

Foreword

Life is full of choices. Men and women choose regularly whether to live life with God or without Him. When we experience a true encounter with God, our perspective and our priorities certainly change. Throughout the Bible, we read the accounts of individuals and their responses to an encounter with God. The struggles we often encounter are a result of our failure to live in *coram Deo,* in the presence and before the eyes of God.

The early church was filled with respect and fear for the Almighty God. In the following pages, you will learn of those who walked with God and those who turned from God. We all need help establishing and maintaining an alignment with God. God has a mission for your life. Are we willing to surrender our will to the will of God, allowing Him to examine our hearts? Will we take intentional steps of faith toward God?

A life that is pleasing to God is one that is truly lived in the presence of God. God grants the humble and faithful with His presence and power to overcome the foolishness to which many succumb. Living with a constant awareness of the presence of God brings victory in faithful living. The world today is full of religions, but seemingly fewer and fewer seek a life of faith that truly pleases God and desire unashamedly to do His will. Repeatedly, we become aware of examples of those who have known God, but recklessly live their lives as if He were not watching.

1

Before God's Face: The Discipline of Coram Deo is a great source of encouragement to prevent us from losing our bearings in this journey of life. We will seek God and find Him when we seek Him with all of our hearts. A life of faith is critical and living in the presence of God is essential. If our life is truly a vapor, a mist that appears and then vanishes quickly, I challenge you to embrace *coram Deo* and live in the presence of God.

Paul Leslie

Senior Minister at McDonough Christian Church

Preface

Happy are those who hear the joyful call to worship, for they will walk in the light of your presence, Lord (Psalm 89:15 NLT).

Like millions of American children born in the 1960's and 1970's, I was regularly taken to church by my parents, which was common if you lived in the South as I did. My family rarely missed a service. This included Sunday school followed by Sunday morning worship, Sunday night worship, midweek Bible study on Wednesday night, vacation Bible school during summer break, and occasional revival meetings. If the church doors opened, my family went. My parents, my three siblings, and I were always among the faithful.

Our church, like any church, had members who were at various levels of commitment. I soon learned the reality of the concept that twenty percent of the congregation did eighty percent of the church work. I think it is fair to say that we were somewhere in the mix of that twenty percent that took serving in the church seriously. My dad was a deacon and a Sunday school teacher, and my mother was the queen of the cradle roll. She knew every little kid in diapers and could tell colorful stories of fond memories about my older siblings' peers when they were in diapers a decade before. She loved taking care of babies. Both my parents were spiritual examples to me and taught me the importance of knowing the Bible and the value of volunteering.

Growing up in the church I also became aware of a few people who were very devoted to serving in church for a while and then sort of faded away. Of course, we had all seen the tabloid news of disgraced TV evangelists caught up in some controversy that alienated their family and their church, but this type of scandal was an anomaly and didn't happen at our church. Usually if someone left the church, it was because he or she either moved away, or started attending another local church because of some offense over a personal matter. Our family experienced occasional strife in the church such as small spats with other members, but it was nothing that ever concerned me. I am eternally grateful for my upbringing with both parents serving in the church.

In my freshman year of college, my world was rocked when, one October day, my dad came home from work, packed his bags, told my mom he wanted a divorce, and walked out. They had been married thirty years. We later discovered Dad had been having an affair with another woman for over a year. He had it all planned out. He waited until I graduated from high school and started college before bailing out. When his opportunity to leave with some semblance of completing the responsibility of raising four children, he left his wife, his youngest son, his home, and his church. It was a nightmare.

As a teenager, I didn't know how to process the betrayal. How does someone walk off like that? How does a committed church leader, father of four, husband of thirty years shed the values he held so dear and leave it all behind? This wasn't just anyone walking away from his family and faith. This was **my dad**, my spiritual mentor, and one of my male role models, not to mention the sole breadwinner of the household. Words cannot express the shock and shame I felt in the fall of 1984. This series of events tested my young faith like nothing else had.

Even now, after thirty years, it baffles me. I have now been married for twenty-eight years, am a father of two and an active servant in the church. My dad's behavior still makes no sense to me. How does someone who had a saving faith in Jesus Christ, who sacrificially served His church for decades, and who brought up his family on the straight-and-narrow just check out as he did?

Have you had similar experiences? I imagine most adults reading this book have probably known people who have abandoned their faith. Maybe you know of a story more dramatic than my dad's story, maybe not. Nevertheless, you have probably known someone whose faith was once strong, and then, over time, wavered in some way. Maybe the person that comes to your mind stopped volunteering and participating and then eventually stopped attending church altogether. Of course, if you ask that person about what happened, he will have an explanation of some sort. It is likely he will say he appreciates your concern but everything is fine. If you are a believer in Jesus Christ, knowing that He died for us, His Bride, how do you get your head around someone having that same knowledge and walking away from the church?

Our discussion is not about questioning someone's salvation. The point is not even for us to investigate or speculate about other church members' lives to see how or why their faith faltered. This book will not debate eternal security, free will, or doctrinal foundations of backsliding. The point is much more practical and pragmatic. The focus is how we, as fully devoted disciples of Christ, can live a life worthy of our calling, protected from gross mistakes like those described, and have an effective Christian walk.

History reveals to us that mankind's past is littered with people who started off knowing God, possessed a deep faith in their Creator, and then somehow lost their bearings. The Bible gives us many examples of people who lost their way, real men and women of faith who witnessed God's power and yet later seemed to contract spiritual amnesia and make huge mistakes. The results were devastating.

This study will look at Bible stories and ask the questions: What can we learn? What is the purpose of certain Bible stories being preserved for all time?

Our study will, for example, consider these stories:

- Adam and Eve

- Moses

- King Saul

- King David

- Jonah

- Simon Peter

All these people of faith knew God. Every one of them witnessed God's power or experienced His presence in some significant way. Yet at a certain point, each of them acted as if God were not present or not watching. The results were painful and sometimes catastrophic.

This study will look at these Bible stories and others using a lens that is the Latin phrase: *coram Deo*. We will examine several Bible stories through the prism of God's presence.

"During the Reformation, 'coram Deo' became the rallying cry for reformers [like Martin Luther] .... [It is a Latin phrase that means] 'in the presence of' or 'before the eyes of God'."[1]

Charles Colson also refers to R.C. Sproul who wrote that nothing marked the Reformation more than the awe of the holy, majestic God that drove the reformers to their knees in fear and reverence. The early church was marked with wonder, holy fear, and reverence (Acts 2:43; 5:11).

What the modern church desperately needs is a realization of God's presence and a new sense of wonderment. We need a healthy dose of the awe (fearful respect) that characterized the early church.

This study will analyze and reflect on a few key biblical stories of men and women of faith, some of whom stumbled and others who serve as our role models. We must learn from their testimony. Their stories have been preserved for us through the ages for a reason. Hebrews 11:4, speaking of the biblical stories of real people of faith, says they "still speak" even though they are dead. We must learn from the stories of victorious people of faith, like Abel, as well as tragic stories of those whose faith faltered, like Cain. As we journey together, this book will expand on the discipline of coram Deo. By putting elements of this discipline into action, we can protect ourselves from spiritual amnesia and other pitfalls, and enhance our walk with Christ. We need to learn to live with the constant awareness of the presence of God and act accordingly. Developing this approach over the past few years has made a big difference in my life, and I pray that it can do the same for you.

As we study the faithful walk of our heroes and heroines of the faith, we should ask ourselves, "Were these not just ordinary people?" As we look at the biblical figures who lost their way, we ought to consider the question, "Are we any better than they?" We are the church, the adopted children of God. In many ways we, too, have lost our way. We all have suffered from spiritual amnesia. We have lost sight of our purpose in the grand scheme of things.

It is my reverent prayer that the advice in this book on living coram Deo will inspire readers to seek God and pursue a closer walk with Him. We must have constant reminders of God's power, His purpose, and His presence in our lives. We need to be motivated to change and to be spurred to action. If only we could live in the constant realization that God is an all-knowing, all-present, and **loving** Father that only wants what is best for us. If only we, as the church, could learn to maintain a sense of God's presence.

7Hear my voice when I call, Lord; be merciful to me and answer me.

8My heart says of you, "Seek his face!" Your face, Lord, I will seek.

9Do not hide your face from me. Do not turn your servant away in anger; you have been my helper. Do not reject me or forsake me, God my Savior (Psalm 27:7-9).

Seeking His face is living coram Deo.

One tenet of this study is that we need help in getting our heads, hearts, and habits aligned with God. The best way I know to do that is for us to learn to dwell in His presence, in the light of His face as if we were literally before Him. I invite you to take this journey with me as together we learn the spiritual discipline of coram Deo.

Overview of the Chapters

	Chapter Title	Scripture	Comments
Chapter 1	God's Design	Genesis 1-3	**Plan:** God's relationship with Adam and Eve in The Garden

Chapter 2	Spiritual Hiding	Genesis 3 and Jonah 1	**Problem:** The Fall of Man, Jonah runs from God's will for his life
Chapter 3	Realization and Response	Various passages	**Perspective:** Jacob, Samuel, Isaiah, and Simon Peter realize God's presence
Chapter 4	God-Forsaken Times	Job and other passages	**Healing:** Dealing with those difficult "God-forsaken" times in our lives
Chapter 5	Renewing Our Minds	Various passages	**Head:** Paul, Martin Luther, getting our minds right
Chapter 6	Transformation	Exodus and Acts	**Heart:** Moses, Saul/Paul, Brother Lawrence; a change of heart
Chapter 7	Our Mission	Various passages	**Habits:** Tending our garden, God's unique calling for each of us
Chapter 8	Spiritual Amnesia	I Samuel, II Samuel	**Head:** King Saul and King David; focus our mind on God
Chapter 9	Serving an Awesome God	Psalm 139	**Heart:** Understanding God's power, a heart for God
Chapter 10	His Presence in Our Present	Various passages	**Habits:** Enoch, Elijah, Psalmist, and Brother Lawrence on our walk
Chapter 11	Carpe Diem and coram Deo	Various passages	**Hurry:** The urgency of living in God's presence every day

All scripture quotations are from the New International Version (NIV) unless specifically noted otherwise.

Chapter 1: God's Design

Introduction

God designed mankind to have a close relationship with Him. We see that clearly in the book of Genesis as God created the world. We read that God chose to make mankind in a unique way: in His image. Adam and Eve enjoyed a special face-to-face relationship with God in the Garden, literally in His presence (true coram Deo). Although God would have special relationships with others throughout history, He revealed His original design for mankind most clearly in the story of Adam and Eve in the Garden. The rest of history can be viewed as God's pursuit of a restored close relationship with fallen mankind, a quest to redeem us from our sin that separated us from Him. God's love fueled this quest so strongly that He sent His only Son, Jesus, who descended to Earth as Immanuel — God with us.

Someone has said that man has an innate need for God that only He can meet or fulfill. Many people today are futilely trying to fill that void with something other than God, which is like trying to force a square peg into a round hole.

In this chapter, we will explore the biblical foundation of God's **special design** for man, God's **unique relationship** with man, and man's **inherent need** for God in his life.

Bible Study

God created man to be special. Many of the intellectuals and scholars of our modern world tell us mankind is no different from the other animals around us except for maybe an opposable thumb and a little more intelligence. However, when we read the creation story, we see a different picture.

God Made Man in His Image

> *24And God said, "Let the land produce living creatures according to their kinds: the livestock, the creatures that move along the ground, and the wild animals, each according to its kind." And it was so. 25God made the wild animals according to their kinds, the livestock according to their kinds, and all the creatures that move along the ground according to their kinds. And God saw that it was good.*
>
> *26Then God said, "Let us make mankind in our image, in our likeness, so that they may rule over the fish in the sea and the birds in the sky, over the livestock and all the wild animals, and over all the creatures that move along the ground."*
>
> *27So God created mankind in his own image, in the image of God he created them; male and female he created them* (Genesis 1:24-27).

God Formed Man from the Dust of the Ground and Breathed Life into Him

> *Then the Lord God formed a man from the dust of the ground and breathed into his nostrils the breath of life, and the man became a living being* (Genesis 2:7).

You see, no matter what the academic world may try to tell us about DNA, genes, and evolution, we can read the truth in the

Holy Scriptures. God created mankind in a special way. God made man in His image, and our Creator breathed life into us unlike any other animal. We are living souls. We have the breath of life and a hint of God's spirit within us.

In addition to God creating mankind in a special way, set apart from the rest of creation by our Creator, He also created and equipped us for a special purpose.

God Gave Man a Special Purpose

28God blessed them and said to them, "Be fruitful and increase in number; fill the earth and subdue it. Rule over the fish in the sea and the birds in the sky and over every living creature that moves on the ground."

29Then God said, "I give you every seed-bearing plant on the face of the whole earth and every tree that has fruit with seed in it. They will be yours for food. 30And to all the beasts of the earth and all the birds in the sky and all the creatures that move along the ground — everything that has the breath of life in it — I give every green plant for food." And it was so.

31God saw all that he had made, and it was very good. And there was evening, and there was morning — the sixth day (Genesis 1:28-31).

8Now the Lord God had planted a garden in the east, in Eden; and there he put the man he had formed. 9And the Lord God made all kinds of trees grow out of the ground — trees that were pleasing to the eye and good for food. In the middle of the garden were the tree of life and the tree of the knowledge of good and evil.

15The Lord God took the man and put him in the Garden of Eden to work it and take care of it (Genesis 2:8, 9, 15).

God blessed man and gave him specific commands to work as God's partners (ref: II Peter 1:4) on this earth. God did **not need** us to tend the garden, nor did He need someone to have dominion over the other creatures. He chose this specific purpose for us and equipped us with everything we needed to accomplish this mission in His divine plan. After God created man in purity, beauty, safety, and innocence, He also prepared a special place for man.

Moreover, in creating man in a special way with a special purpose: He gifted us with free will.

God Gave Man a Choice of Obedience to Him

> [15]*The Lord God took the man and put him in the Garden of Eden to work it and take care of it.* [16]*And the Lord God commanded the man, "You are free to eat from any tree in the garden;* [17]*but you must not eat from the tree of the knowledge of good and evil, for when you eat from it you will certainly die"*(Genesis 2:15-17).

This is somewhat incredible and sometimes hard to understand; it is the concept of human free will in the context of God's sovereignty. He does not need man, yet He chose to make us partners in His creation. He could force man to obey Him, yet He allowed us to make our own choices. He knew that man would sin and fall from grace, yet He still chose to carry out His design.

We see God's design in the story of Adam and Eve. His design was for an intimate, face-to-face relationship with Him, but He also gave them one simple restriction: Do not eat of one particular tree. God set specific limits on man, giving him freewill in order to test his heart. We will discuss this fact further in chapter 2.

In the first portion of Genesis (1:1-2:3) during the basic creation narrative, the name used for God is the generic name *Elohim*.

Ann Spangler's book *Praying the Names of God* explains this name for God is the most ancient designation for God. The name is pronounced e-lo-HEEM and is plural of the name *El*, a name used for God in several ancient cultures. This plural form of the name *El* is not to indicate more than one god but is used to emphasize the majesty and complexity of the one true Mighty Creator God.[2] This may also hint at the concept of the Trinity. It is used in many places in Genesis and throughout the Hebrew Holy Scriptures to remind us of His power, creativity, and sovereignty.

Genesis chapter 2 implies a special relationship when the Holy Spirit inspired Moses to use a different, more specific name for God. In 2:4 and 2:7, the name Yahweh (YHWH) is used (Jehovah) when describing man in detail. Dr. Merrill Unger, author of *Unger's Bible Handbook*, says this word indicates a "'special revelatory ... relationship' between Jehovah and man."[3] Dr. Henry H. Halley, Bible scholar and author of *Halley's Bible Handbook*, says basically the same thing, that *Jehovah* was God's personal name; He was sharing part of His identity with Adam and Eve in Genesis 2.[4]

We see God reveal more of Himself as He speaks to Moses, who asks,

> [13]*But Moses said to God, "Suppose I go to the Israelites and say to them, 'The God of your fathers has sent me to you' and they ask me, 'What is His name?' Then what shall I tell them?"* [14]*God said to Moses, "I AM WHO I AM. This is what you are to say to the Israelites: 'I AM has sent me to you'"* [15]*God also said to Moses, "... This is my name forever, the name by which I am to be remembered from generation to generation"* (Exodus 3:13-15).

Our God is the great I AM! What an amazingly simple way to express an astoundingly complex truth. In this life, we may not fully understand the intricacies of the Trinity or fully appreciate the intimate relationship that God had with Adam and Eve, but we should understand that He loves us. Jesus called Him Abba Father, which is an intimate name like a child saying, "Daddy." I think we can at least understand that our relationship with God should be very much like a loving father with his children. Imagine what that must have been like for Adam and Eve.

God Allowed Man to Name all the Animals

19Now the Lord God had formed out of the ground all the wild animals and all the birds in the sky. He brought them to the man to see what he would name them; and whatever the man called each living creature, that was its name. 20So the man gave names to all the livestock, the birds in the sky and all the wild animals (Genesis 2:19-20a).

Try to put yourself in Adam's place for a moment. This is an incredible picture, the forever-existing, all-powerful "I AM" passing responsibility, trust, confidence, and love to the created man, Adam. God, the loving Father and Creator of the universe, chose to spend quality time with the child He loves. The Father brought the animals to him, giving Adam the authority and privilege to name every one of them. Can you imagine what that must have been like? It is truly experiencing life together, God and man in a close relationship.

We get a hint of a similar picture if we read between the lines, so to speak, in the next chapter of Genesis.

Adam and Eve Knew the Sound of God in the Garden

8Then the man and his wife heard the sound of the Lord God as He was walking in the garden in the cool of the day, and they hid from the Lord God among the trees of the garden. 9But the Lord God called to the man, "Where are you?" 10He answered, "I heard you in the garden, and I was afraid because I was naked; so I hid" (Genesis 3:8-10).

Based on the wording, God habitually walked in the Garden with Adam and Eve. This was truly an intimate, face-to-face relationship. They were accustomed to walking together in the garden with their Creator. Stephen Miller, author of *The Complete Guide to the Bible*, describes the relationship before The Fall as an "intimate relationship between God and humanity." Miller goes on to say, "Once upon a time, Adam and Eve had recognized the sound of God's footsteps, apparently because he spent time with them 'walking in the garden' regularly."[5]

What a beautiful picture of fellowship between God and mankind!

Therefore, we see from the first few chapters of Genesis that God designed mankind to be special and designed us for an intimate relationship with Him. This is why today we say we have a *God-shaped hole* that only God can fill.

Have you ever wondered where that phrase came from? Is it biblical? Where did the phrase God-shaped hole originate?

Blaise Pascal, a 17th Century Christian apologist and world-renowned mathematician, is often quoted as saying something like, "There is a God-shaped vacuum in the heart of every person, and it can never be filled by any created thing. It can only be filled by God, made known through Jesus Christ." However, based on my research, the actual quote found in Blaise Pascal's book *Pensees*, is even more verbose and eloquent (as you might expect from 17th Century prose).

> "What is it then that this desire and this inability proclaim to us, but that there was once in man a true happiness of which there now remain to him only the mark and empty

trace, which he in vain tries to fill from all his surroundings, seeking from things absent the help he does not obtain in things present? But these are all inadequate, because the **infinite abyss** can only be filled by an infinite and immutable object, that is to say, only by God Himself ..." (emphasis mine).[6]

Perhaps Pascal was influenced by other early Christian writers such as Augustine (St. Augustine of Hippo), who wrote in his *Confessions*, "Thou awakest us to delight in Thy praise; for Thou madest us for Thyself, and our heart is restless, until it repose in Thee."[7]

A writer from our modern times also expressed this concept. In his book, *Mere Christianity*, C.S. Lewis wrote, "If I find in myself a desire which no experience in this world can satisfy, the most probable explanation is that I was made for another world."[8]

This speaks of our inner desire that is unsatisfied by this world. When we try to fill that void with something other than a close relationship with God, as Pascal said, we are trying in vain to fill an infinite abyss with **present things**. This is like trying to put a square peg into a round hole.

For further study, consider other faithful people who had a similar face-to-face relationship with our Creator:

- Noah (Genesis 6:5-14)

- Abraham (Gen. 17:1-5)

- Moses (Exodus 33:11; Numbers 12:8)

There are other proofs or strong arguments in favor of the concept of a God-shaped hole in anthropology. In virtually every major culture in history, people have believed in something bigger than themselves, typically in a creator of the universe.

Virtually every culture has believed in some form of a god or gods including Native Americans, Aborigines, ancient Greeks, ancient Romans, ancient Nordics, Hindus, native Africans, ancient Egyptians, and others (ref: Acts 17: 22-27 and Romans 1:19-20).

But is the concept of a God-shaped hole biblical? I think we find the biblical basis in the gospel of John:

> *37Now on the last day, the great day of the feast, Jesus stood and cried out, saying, "If any man is thirsty, let him come to Me and drink. 38"He who believes in Me, as the Scripture said, 'From his innermost being shall flow rivers of living water.'" 39But this He spoke of the Spirit, whom those who believed in Him were to receive; for the Spirit was not yet given, because Jesus was not yet glorified* (John 7:37-39 NASB).

The phrase "innermost being" is from the Greek root word *koilos*, meaning hole or empty place.[9] It is often translated belly or womb but figuratively means the innermost part of a man, the soul, heart, as the seat of thought, feeling, and choice. In John 7, Jesus is describing a spiritual empty place in the heart of man, not a physical belly or womb. This spiritual empty place is the source of our spiritual thirst. The divine solution to this thirst is to fill it with living water from the Holy Spirit.

You may say, "So what? I already knew most of this." However, knowing is different from living. Believing is not enough. James said that even the demons believe and tremble (James 2:19). God calls us to a living and active faith.

Ponder the main points of this chapter: God's **special design** for man, God's **unique relationship** with man, and our **inherent need** for God in our lives. Does your lifestyle reflect that reality? Are you living a life worthy of this high calling? Do you have an intimate relationship with God where you spend time with Him, filling your empty space with all of Him?

If you are satisfied with your spiritual maturity, you may decide that parts of this book are more of a nice reminder. But if you are like the rest of us and find your spiritual life is characterized by disappointment, frustration, and a desire for a deeper relationship with God, then the rest of this book is for you.

At the end of each chapter, there will be a life-change challenge to make this a practical study, not just theoretical. Just before the challenge, there is a section on application. Before those two sections, we take time to pause for a few moments and look carefully at a brief scripture or two that speaks to the chapter theme. Then after devoting some time to the scripture, we will look to the chapter application and challenge.

Devotional Scripture

The following passage speaks to God's great design for mankind. God desires a restored relationship with His children. He wants us to revere Him and have a sense of awe and wonder as we dwell in His presence. Please carefully consider and meditate on this Bible passage:

> *⁹What do workers gain from their toil? ¹⁰I have seen the burden God has laid on the human race. ¹¹He has made everything beautiful in its time. He has also set eternity in the human heart; yet no one can fathom what God has done from beginning to end. ¹²I know that there is nothing better for people than to be happy and to do good while they live. ¹³That each of them may eat and drink, and find satisfaction in all their toil — this is the gift of God. ¹⁴I know that everything God does will endure forever; nothing can be added to it and nothing taken from it. God does it so that people will fear him* (Ecclesiastes 3:9-14).

Some Bible translations have a footnote that indicates an alternate rendering of the language for that last phrase in verse 14 could be *"be in awe before Him"* (NASB). I believe the Amplified Bible translation best expresses God's heart in this matter:

> *I know that whatever God does, it endures forever; nothing can be added to it nor anything taken from it. And God does it so that men will [reverently] fear Him [revere and worship Him, knowing that He is]* (AMP).

This passage speaks of God's intentional design for mankind. His design is for us to have a reverent sense of awe and fear of Him, but also to have a close relationship with our heavenly Father just as Adam and Eve originally had with Him in the Garden.

Life-Change Challenge

As Christians, we are destined to a restored face-to-face relationship with God. Of course, I am speaking of our eternal salvation when we will behold God's face and truly experience coram Deo. In this life, we are separated from God by sin; but we don't have to settle for a distant relationship with God. He loves His children very much and wants us to draw near to Him. We need to imitate Jesus Christ. We need to grasp the reality that, as Christians, the Holy Spirit indwells us and we are before God's face all the time. But our minds easily forget. The discipline of coram Deo laid out in the chapters ahead can help.

Rather than this study being purely academic, let it challenge you. Our first life-change challenge is to start with genuine, heartfelt prayer. Let's spend some additional time daily in prayer. This does not have to be complicated at all, and our prayers don't need to be long and elaborate. Use the Lord's Prayer as a simple structure:

⁹[Jesus said] This, then, is how you should pray:

"Our Father in heaven, hallowed be your name,

¹⁰your kingdom come, your will be done, on earth as it is in heaven.

¹¹Give us today our daily bread.

¹²And forgive us our debts, as we also have forgiven our debtors.

¹³And lead us not into temptation, but deliver us from the evil one" (Matthew 6:9-13).

In addition to asking for daily bread, as part of the discipline of coram Deo, ask your Father to show you how He has made you unique and special. When you pray, ask Him to reveal to you His **special design** for you. Ask Him to help you understand that He wants to have a **unique and close relationship** with you. Pray for your heart to become aware of your own **inherent need** to experience God in your everyday life.

How can we fill that God-shaped hole with Him and only Him? The goal is for us to open up a constant line of communication with our Father and to pursue a sustained, closer relationship with Him. This must become our new lifestyle, not a temporary success or a one-time, mountaintop experience. A key element of living coram Deo is a genuine thirst for a close relationship with Him.

What do you think is God's great desire for us? What is His design for you? What can you do right now to reconcile with your Father? Ask yourself, "How am I going to live differently? What is God calling me to do?"

Pray for God to answer these questions for you. Based on the history revealed in the Holy Scriptures, God's overall desire is to reconcile and restore our broken relationship with Him so that we can have an intimate relationship with Him now and forever.

A common adage says that it takes at least twenty-one days to establish a habit. Will you dedicate yourself to pray for a closer walk with Him at least once a day for twenty-one days in a row? This is the first step toward pursuing God's original design for us in the context of coram Deo. When we are in prayer, we are **before the face of God.** Let's accept this prayer challenge together! With God's help, we are more than conquerors (Romans 8:39).

Looking Forward

Now that we are clear on God's original plan, we will explore the real problem, the idea of *spiritual hiding*. This can occur when we are in denial about our own sin or when we literally run away from what we know is God's plan for us. We are going to study The Fall of Man (Genesis 3) and the plight of Jonah (Jonah 1).

Chapter 2: Spiritual Hiding

Introduction

This chapter will explore two examples of spiritual hiding in biblical history: Adam and Eve (actually hiding from God in the Garden); and the prophet Jonah (running from God's calling). We can learn from these biblical struggles with sin and apply the lessons learned to our own walk.

John Ortberg retells a story (originally told by Dallas Willard) about a two-year-old girl in her grandmother's backyard who discovered the "secret" of making mud. Her grandmother had been reading and facing away from the child. When the grandmother saw the mess, she scolded the little girl, took her inside, and cleaned her up. Then the grandmother told the little girl not to make any more mud. Soon the grandmother stopped paying attention again and the girl returned to her newfound recipe. This time, she posed a sweetly worded request: "Don't look at me, Nana. Okay?"[10]

Ortberg makes the point that the heart of this two-year-old lives in every person. We want our way and do not want anyone telling us what to do. Her desire to do what she wants outside the view of her authority figure is symbolic of our own stubborn heart. Ortberg quotes Willard who writes, "This shows us how necessary it is to us that we be unobserved in our wrong."[11]

Jesus understood the principle well. When Nicodemus came to Him under the cover of darkness, Jesus mentioned this concept:

> *¹⁹This is the verdict: Light has come into the world, but men loved darkness instead of light because their deeds were evil. ²⁰Everyone who does evil hates the light, and will not come into the light for fear that his deeds will be exposed* (John 3:19-20).

Can you think of a time when you were younger when you, like this two-year-old, tried to hide your mischief? Maybe you covered up something you broke or a lie you told. Are we that different from this little girl in the way we respond to authority? How different are we from the biblical figures we are about to study?

Bible Study

The Fall of Man

> *²⁵Adam and his wife were both naked, and they felt no shame.*
>
> *¹Now the serpent was more crafty than any of the wild animals the Lord God had made. He said to the woman, "Did God really say, 'You must not eat from any tree in the garden'?"*
>
> *²The woman said to the serpent, "We may eat fruit from the trees in the garden, ³but God did say, 'You must not eat fruit from the tree that is in the middle of the garden, and you must not touch it, or you will die.'"*
>
> *⁴"You will not certainly die," the serpent said to the woman. ⁵"For God knows that when you eat from it your eyes will be opened, and you will be like God, knowing good and evil."*

6 When the woman saw that the fruit of the tree was good for food and pleasing to the eye, and also desirable for gaining wisdom, she took some and ate it. She also gave some to her husband, who was with her, and he ate it. 7Then the eyes of both of them were opened, and they realized they were naked; so they sewed fig leaves together and made coverings for themselves.

8Then the man and his wife heard the sound of the Lord God as he was walking in the garden in the cool of the day, and they hid from the Lord God among the trees of the garden. 9But the Lord God called to the man, "Where are you?"

10He answered, "I heard you in the garden, and I was afraid because I was naked; so I hid."

11And he said, "Who told you that you were naked? Have you eaten from the tree that I commanded you not to eat from?"

12The man said, "The woman you put here with me — she gave me some fruit from the tree, and I ate it."

13Then the Lord God said to the woman, "What is this you have done?" The woman said, "The serpent deceived me, and I ate" (Genesis 2:25 – 3:13).

In a way, Adam and Eve were acting like the little two-year-old that said, "Don't look at me." They tried to hide from God because they were afraid and ashamed.

Ortberg describes this human behavior like this, "Any time we choose to do wrong or to withhold doing right, we choose **hiddenness** as well ...."[12]

It is as if Adam and Eve were saying, "Don't look at me, God. I heard you in the garden, and I was afraid, so I hid. God, don't look at me."

A. W. Tozer wrote:

> "Adam sinned and in his panic, frantically tried to do the impossible: He tried to hide from the Presence of God. David also must have had wild thoughts of trying to escape from the Presence, for he wrote, 'Whither shall I go from thy spirit? Or whither shall I flee from thy presence?' [But in truth, David knew] that God's being and God's seeing are the same [and there is no escaping or hiding from God]."13

We know that we cannot hide from God. Yet, by our actions, sometimes we are in fact trying to hide from God. We may not say, "Don't look at me God." But we might think, "I'll just do this and then ask for forgiveness later." This is just like saying, "God don't look right now; leave me alone for a little while; look the other way for now; then I'll ask for Your forgiveness." That is in essence the same thing. When we choose sin, we are also choosing to try to hide from God. I think this breaks the heart of our loving Father.

Adam and Eve were not the only people ever to try to hide from God. One of the most obvious examples of a man hiding or running from God was Jonah.

Jonah Runs from God

1The word of the Lord came to Jonah son of Amittai: 2"Go to the great city of Nineveh and preach against it, because its wickedness has come up before me."

3But Jonah ran away from the Lord and headed for Tarshish. He went down to Joppa, where he found a ship bound for that port. After paying the fare, he went aboard and sailed for Tarshish to flee from the Lord.

4Then the Lord sent a great wind on the sea, and such a violent storm arose that the ship threatened to break up.

5All the sailors were afraid and each cried out to his own god. And they threw the cargo into the sea to lighten the ship.

But Jonah had gone below deck, where he lay down and fell into a deep sleep. 6The captain went to him and said, "How can you sleep? Get up and call on your god! Maybe he will take notice of us so that we will not perish."

7Then the sailors said to each other, "Come, let us cast lots to find out who is responsible for this calamity." They cast lots and the lot fell on Jonah. 8So they asked him, "Tell us, who is responsible for making all this trouble for us? What kind of work do you do? Where do you come from? What is your country? From what people are you?"

9He answered, "I am a Hebrew and I worship the Lord, the God of heaven, who made the sea and the dry land."

10This terrified them and they asked, "What have you done?" (They knew he was running away from the Lord, because he had already told them so.)

11The sea was getting rougher and rougher. So they asked him, "What should we do to you to make the sea calm down for us?"

12"Pick me up and throw me into the sea," he replied, "and it will become calm. I know that it is my fault that this great storm has come upon you."

13Instead, the men did their best to row back to land. But they could not, for the sea grew even wilder than before. 14Then they cried out to the Lord, "Please, Lord, do not let us die for taking this man's life. Do not hold us accountable for killing an innocent man, for you, Lord, have done as you pleased." 15Then they took Jonah and threw him overboard, and the raging sea grew calm. ¹⁶At this the men greatly feared the Lord, and they offered a sacrifice to the Lord and made vows to him.

¹⁷Now the Lord provided a huge fish to swallow Jonah, and Jonah was in the belly of the fish three days and three nights (Jonah 1:1-17).

Jonah was not exactly trying to hide from God as much as he was trying not to obey God by running away. In this situation, God wanted Jonah to go to Nineveh, a primary city of Israel's enemy. Jonah wanted to stay as far away from that city as he could, so he tried to run from God to avoid His plans for him. Jonah had chosen hiddenness. I am fairly certain Jonah did not choose the fish portion of that hiddenness. That was God's masterful touch to this epic story. Now Sunday school classes and their teachers are eternally grateful.

Don't we do the same thing as Jonah? We hear a good lesson or sermon and feel convicted in that moment, but we procrastinate and don't take any action. We mean well but never get around to doing the very thing we wanted to do when the Holy Spirit tugged at our hearts.

Perhaps it is more obvious than that. Maybe we feel our conscience telling us to do something and we start making excuses. We justify not doing it because we don't feel like doing anything and we push back.

Max Lucado wrote that this attitude and behavior is comparable to "My Way" sung by Frank Sinatra. It is rooted in our stubborn spirit, which is part of human nature.

- All I needed to do was apologize, but I had to argue.

- All I needed to do was listen, but I had to open my big mouth.

- All I needed to do was be patient, but I had to take control.

- All I needed to do was give it to God, but I had to try to fix it myself ...

- I don't need advice ...

- I can handle this myself ... Can you relate?[14]

On and on we can go with a whole litany of actions we may take that we will regret later. We may be blatantly hiding from God or we might be running from God, or we might be just procrastinating. Perhaps we are justifying doing nothing. Maybe we are trying to take control to do it "my way."

In the end, we are choosing hiddenness. We are rejecting our close relationship with God. As Tozer wrote, we are trying to do the impossible if we are trying to hide from the presence of God. The root problem is the same: sin and rebellion.

Deception, disrespect, and betrayal damage relationships. We know it to be true in human relationships. Love, respect, and trust are the things that build strong marriages. Couples that experience unfaithfulness or mistreatment suffer from a damaged relationship.

"In the same manner that human relationships are sustained by openness and honesty, so it is also with our relationship with God. When we sin against Him, we unconsciously erect a barrier between Heaven and ourselves. We may still go to church, but a sense of distance and artificiality emerges in our hearts.

"Each of those defenses we have erected to keep God out ultimately walls us in, spiritually imprisoning us in our sins. These barriers degenerate into strongholds of demonic oppression. Eventually our walls toward God imprison us outside the Divine Presence, trapping the soul in outer darkness."[15]

That sounds a little bit like Hell, doesn't it?

Devotional Scripture

Before we dive into the application and challenge sections of the chapter, let's pause for a moment and reflect. The theme of this chapter is the problem of spiritual hiding. The opposite of hiding is seeking. Take a few moments to devote your full attention to the meaning of the following two scriptures:

> *You will seek me and find me when you seek me with all your heart* (Jeremiah 29:13).

> *[26]From one man he made all the nations, that they should inhabit the whole earth; and he marked out their appointed times in history and the boundaries of their lands. [27]God did this so that they would seek him and perhaps reach out for him and find him, though he is not far from any one of us. [28]For in him we live and move and have our being*
> (Acts 17:26-28a).

These two passages speak to God's desire for us to seek Him with all of our heart. This is in stark contrast to Adam, Eve, and Jonah who, at one time in their lives, chose to hide from God rather than seek Him. All true believers should seek God. Seeking God is a foundational principle of coram Deo. Another major tenet of the discipline of coram Deo is the last phrase in the passage above, "in Him we live and move and have our being." That is our aim, to learn that we literally live and have our very being in Him every day.

Application/Implication

As we have seen, sin separates us from the presence of God just as sin forced Adam and Eve to flee the Garden and lose their face-to-face relationship with God.

What do you think about the idea of spiritual hiding? As you reflect on the plight of Adam and Eve, as well as Jonah, what can you learn? Are you any different? Could the spiritual discipline of coram Deo help you when you feel the need to hide from God?

Consider this statement (paraphrase from Ortberg), "No matter how small, every choice to sin or choice to hide from God WILL diminish our ability to experience God's presence."[16]

How do people try to hide from God today? How do people run from God today?

In light of these biblical accounts of spiritual hiding, what is our attitude toward sin today? Do we take it seriously? Do we really grasp the full impact and scope of sin? Stephen Miller wrote that, after The Fall, nothing was ever the same and "the rest of the Bible is the story of God working to correct the damage and to defeat sin."[17]

Matthew Henry's commentary on The Fall said, "Those who by sin go astray ... should seriously consider where they are .... [They are] in bondage to Satan [and on the] road to utter ruin ..." when they try to hide from God.[18] Sin is a serious matter our modern society winks at and sometimes even glamorizes. God calls us to a higher standard.

Reflecting on this chapter on spiritual hiding, consider how you can get rid of barriers that obstruct your sense of God's presence. How are you running or avoiding His will for your life? How can you be more content and conscious of His presence? What will you choose, hide or seek?

Life-Change Challenge

In our modern American society of political correctness and multi-cultural sensitivity, we have pushed thoughts and words about God out of our daily lives. Rather than hiding from God, we should choose to seek God. Psalm 19:1-2 says:

¹The heavens declare the glory of God; the skies proclaim the work of his hands.

²Day after day they pour forth speech; night after night they reveal knowledge.

G. M. Hopkins was a 19th Century English poet and Jesuit priest. In a poem titled "God's Grandeur" he wrote, "The world is charged with the grandeur of God."[19]

Psalm 19 is telling us that God's creation is a constant reminder of His presence. Hopkins' was paying tribute to the grandeur of God's creation. Are we aware of this, or are we so distracted that we don't sense His grandeur?

During the timeframe I originally wrote this Bible study (2013), I was leaving work in downtown Atlanta and on my way home after dark. As I rounded a corner, I saw an animal suddenly crossing the road. Fortunately, I was not driving fast and was able to stop with twenty or thirty feet to spare. My headlights perfectly illuminated a work of art: a beautiful gray fox. The headlights lit up his furry coat so it almost glowed. This was an unexpected appearance compliments of my loving Father. The fox paused in the road to look at me long enough that I could appreciate all its features: The large ears, the pointed nose, the thick fur, and the huge fluffy tail. Then, as suddenly as it ran in front of me, it darted back into the underbrush and out of sight.

In moments like this, I get an overwhelming feeling of thankfulness as I sense God's presence. Something about seeing wildlife in the suburbs makes me feel close to God. I feel so blessed by His handiwork. It always reminds me how delicate life is and how glorious His creation is all around us.

For our life-change challenge for this chapter, look for examples of God's creation in your day-to-day experiences. The world is truly "charged with the grandeur of God." In addition, as part of this challenge and the discipline of coram Deo, I suggest that you journal these encounters. If you are not a person who enjoys journaling, consider at least making a mental note and remembering these moments in your daily prayers. As the psalmist wrote, nature pours out speech about our Creator. I am convinced reminders of His presence will draw you closer to God.

Consider ways to remove barriers that blind you to His presence so you can be on the alert for sudden or unexpected appearances of God's glory and grandeur. It might be as simple as observing a bird digging for worms or a beautiful sunset. Remember to look for divine glimpses of God in people who are all made in His image. View everything you experience in the context of God's presence: **coram Deo.**

Keep up your routine from the last challenge. Pray a simple prayer for God to help you see, feel, and know His presence and to know how God fills our void. Keep the lines of communication with God active every day and throughout your day. The generally accepted advice is that it takes at least three weeks to establish a habit. One recent study indicated that it takes between 18 and 254 days to establish a truly automatic habit.[20]

So keep up the routine until it becomes natural. Add to your prayers a request for God to reveal areas of your life where you can avoid spiritual hiding and start choosing to seek Him instead.

Looking Forward

Now that we have looked at God's plan and His design for mankind and seen the problem with sin and hiddenness, we are going to explore some biblical case studies of how people of faith behaved when they realized they were in the presence of God. Micah 6:6-8 teaches us to come before the Lord in humility and obedience. The case studies we will study next will help us understand our proper response when we acknowledge Him and come into His presence.

Chapter 3: Realization and Response

In this chapter, we will explore several biblical stories of believers who had encounters with God's presence. Studying their reactions in these situations is informative to us as Christians when we consider the appropriate response to His presence. We will use these as case studies as we begin to **realize** God's omnipresence and understand our proper **response**.

Introduction

Rich Mullins was a contemporary Christian songwriter, poet, musician, and artist. He wrote award-winning songs such as "Awesome God," "Sometimes by Step," and "Boy like Me, Man like You." His music career and ministry allowed him to tour not only the U.S. but also all over the world.

My wife Terri and I are huge Rich Mullins fans. In the early 1990's, he was on a European tour which included Amsterdam. Upon his return, during a U.S. concert tour, we heard Rich give his testimony as he openly shared a story of his struggles. Based on my own memory and piecing it together with several online quotations, here is a paraphrase of what he said.

> "In Amsterdam, I just became really keenly and uncomfortably aware that there was so much sin all around us. You think you're growing as a Christian and all of a sudden, you're in a situation. I realized I am still susceptible to sin. After years of behaving myself as best I could, I was

really having to hang on for dear life. I was thinking, 'No one would know.' Fortunately, because I travel with my friend, Beaker, and because he's not afraid to hold me accountable, I didn't do anything. But I sure felt the temptation to toss out my morals for an evening.

"A few days later, in Germany, Beaker and I were sitting on a bench in a train station talking about the whole thing — kind of where we were and where we wanted to be — and we'd gotten into some pretty explicit detail about the nature of our temptations and of those struggles. We were assuming that nobody would be interested enough in whatever we would have to say to actually bother to translate and listen. And this guy leans over — the only other guy in there — and says, 'Excuse me, but are you Rich Mullins?'"[21]

In the concert my wife and I attended, Mullins just paused here for a moment and then said, "Wow...." The audience laughed nervously. He went on to say, "I had to stop for a minute and think back over our conversation to see if I was or not." Then he decided and said, "Yep, I am Rich Mullins. Whether I like myself or not, that's who I am."

Rich Mullins had a gift for being transparent without being too self-deprecating. He summarized by saying, "I think the conclusion of the matter for me is that I do **not** have some kind of illusion of moral superiority. Not that I don't want to be morally excellent." He meant that his faith was **not** rooted in the idea of being more moral than anybody else. "My faith is in the idea that God and His love, mercy and grace are greater than whatever sins any of us commit."

Mullins was not expecting to be in the presence of someone who knew him or knew who he was. He thought he was in the presence of only strangers, but he got a surprise.

Bible Study

Let's read a story about Jacob and the surprise he experienced when he suddenly realized he was in God's presence:

> *¹⁰Jacob left Beersheba and set out for Harran. ¹¹When he reached a certain place, he stopped for the night because the sun had set. Taking one of the stones there, he put it under his head and lay down to sleep. ¹²He had a dream in which he saw a stairway resting on the earth, with its top reaching to heaven, and the angels of God were ascending and descending on it. ¹³There above it stood the Lord, and he said: "I am the Lord, the God of your father Abraham and the God of Isaac. I will give you and your descendants the land on which you are lying. ¹⁴Your descendants will be like the dust of the earth, and you will spread out to the west and to the east, to the north and to the south. All peoples on earth will be blessed through you and your offspring. ¹⁵I am with you and will watch over you wherever you go, and I will bring you back to this land. I will not leave you until I have done what I have promised you."*

> *¹⁶When Jacob awoke from his sleep, he thought, "Surely the Lord is in this place, and I was not aware of it." ¹⁷He was afraid and said, "How awesome is this place! This is none other than the house of God; this is the gate of heaven."*

> *¹⁸Early the next morning Jacob took the stone he had placed under his head and set it up as a pillar and poured oil on top of it. ¹⁹He called that place Bethel, though the city used to be called Luz.*

> *²⁰Then Jacob made a vow saying, "If God will be with me and will watch over me on this journey I am taking and will give me food to eat and clothes to wear ²¹so that I return safely to my father's household, then the Lord will be my God ²²and*

this stone that I have set up as a pillar will be God's house, and of all that you give me I will give you a tenth" (Genesis 28:10-22).

This story becomes our first case study as we consider reactions to God's presence. It is not an ideal scenario. Jacob is not yet ready to completely commit his entire life to God.

Analyze carefully the words Jacob uses: *"If God will be with me [then] the Lord will be my God [and] I will give you a tenth."* Jacob does not yet fully trust God, but this encounter changes his perspective. As time goes by, this encounter will prove to be the beginning of a turning point in his life. A few chapters later, God changes Jacob's name to Israel and the rest is history.

Perhaps a better example for us of someone who had a realization of God's presence and a more admirable response is the calling of Samuel.

[1]The boy Samuel ministered before the Lord under Eli. In those days the word of the Lord was rare; there were not many visions.

[2]One night Eli, whose eyes were becoming so weak that he could barely see, was lying down in his usual place. [3]The lamp of God had not yet gone out, and Samuel was lying down in the house of the Lord, where the ark of God was. [4]Then the Lord called Samuel.

Samuel answered, "Here I am."

[5]And he ran to Eli and said, "Here I am; you called me."

But Eli said, "I did not call; go back and lie down." So he went and lay down.

[6]Again the Lord called, "Samuel!" And Samuel got up and went to Eli and said, "Here I am; you called me."

"My son," Eli said, "I did not call; go back and lie down."

⁷Now Samuel did not yet know the Lord: The word of the Lord had not yet been revealed to him.

⁸A third time the Lord called, "Samuel!" And Samuel got up and went to Eli and said, "Here I am; you called me."

Then Eli realized that the Lord was calling the boy. ⁹So Eli told Samuel, "Go and lie down, and if he calls you, say, 'Speak, Lord, for your servant is listening.'" So Samuel went and lay down in his place.

¹⁰The Lord came and stood there, calling as at the other times, "Samuel! Samuel!"

Then Samuel said, "Speak, for your servant is listening."

¹¹And the Lord said to Samuel: "See, I am about to do something in Israel that will make the ears of everyone who hears about it tingle. ¹²At that time I will carry out against Eli everything I spoke against his family — from beginning to end. ¹³For I told him that I would judge his family forever because of the sin he knew about; his sons blasphemed God, and he failed to restrain them. ¹⁴Therefore I swore to the house of Eli, 'The guilt of Eli's house will never be atoned for by sacrifice or offering.'"

¹⁵Samuel lay down until morning and then opened the doors of the house of the Lord. He was afraid to tell Eli the vision, ¹⁶but Eli called him and said, "Samuel, my son."

Samuel answered, "Here I am."

¹⁷"What was it he said to you?" Eli asked. "Do not hide it from me. May God deal with you, be it ever so severely, if you hide from me anything he told you." ¹⁸So Samuel told him everything, hiding nothing from him. Then Eli said, "He

is the Lord; let him do what is good in his eyes"
(I Samuel 3:1-18).

Notice Samuel's humility and obedient spirit, calling himself God's "servant." Samuel didn't have an issue when his night was interrupted, whether he thought it was Eli or God. Samuel's realization and response to God's calling is an example that we should mirror in our own lives.

Unlike Samuel, sometimes we are busy with our own lives and we do not like interruptions by anyone. Sometimes the tasks that we put as our highest priority are good things: family, duty, church ministry. But we have to be attentive that we are God's servants, and it is God's agenda we need to be following.

Dietrich Bonhoeffer said, "We must be ready to allow ourselves to be interrupted by God."[22]

This is such good advice because anyone who has served in ministry knows that we will encounter people who will test our patience, drain us of our energy, and frustrate our plans. In those instances, we have to be attentive to God's calling to serve sacrificially and appreciate that serving others is what He calls us to do. We must be ready for God to interrupt our plans and our agenda with opportunities to serve His Kingdom.

Solomon gives us good advice about coming into the presence of the Lord.

> *[1]Guard your steps when you go to the house of God. Go near to listen rather than to offer the sacrifice of fools, who do not know that they do wrong.*

> *[2]Do not be quick with your mouth, do not be hasty in your heart to utter anything before God. God is in heaven and you are on earth, so let your words be few.*

3A dream comes when there are many cares, and many words mark the speech of a fool.

7Much dreaming and many words are meaningless. Therefore fear God (Ecclesiastes 5:1-3; 7).

Solomon was giving us wise counsel: Watch what you say, listen more than you speak, and **stand in awe of God**.

As mentioned in the preface, Charles Colson reminds us that the early church was strengthened and encouraged by living in the fear and awe of the Lord, showing great **reverence** for the Almighty (ref: Acts 2:43; 5:11; 9:31). Colson writes, "How desperately the church today needs to take hold of that awe! To understand that we live day by day in the presence of God, that in truth we live each minute, each instant, not knowing whether in the next we will meet Him face to face. Coram Deo. Filled with this holy fear and **reverence**, the early church changed the world" (emphasis mine).[23]

Perhaps the ideal case study for realization and proper response to God's presence can be found in the responses of Isaiah and Simon Peter in the following two passages. First, let's look at Isaiah:

1In the year that King Uzziah died, I saw the Lord, high and exalted, seated on a throne; and the train of his robe filled the temple. 2Above him were seraphim, each with six wings: With two wings they covered their faces, with two they covered their feet, and with two they were flying. 3And they were calling to one another:

"Holy, holy, holy is the Lord Almighty; the whole earth is full of his glory."

4At the sound of their voices the doorposts and thresholds shook and the temple was filled with smoke.

5"Woe to me!" I cried. "I am ruined! For I am a man of unclean lips, and I live among a people of unclean lips, and my eyes have seen the King, the Lord Almighty."

6Then one of the seraphim flew to me with a live coal in his hand, which he had taken with tongs from the altar. 7With it he touched my mouth and said, "See, this has touched your lips; your guilt is taken away and your sin atoned for."

8Then I heard the voice of the Lord saying, "Whom shall I send? And who will go for us?" And I said, "Here am I. Send me!" (Isaiah 6:1-8).

This particular passage is powerful and serves as an excellent illustration for how we should respond to the presence of God who is holy. Francis Chan, minister and best-selling author, has shared his testimony in several conferences. He said that he realized that one day he would come before the Lord just as Isaiah describes. This was a humbling and sobering thought that really resonated with Chan. He goes so far as to say that this particular passage of Isaiah literally changed his life.

My hope is that the concept of living in God's presence will have this same effect on each one of us. Truly comprehending this idea and keeping it in the forefront of our mind is an incredibly powerful spiritual discipline that completely changes our perspective and sets us up for success as a disciple of Christ.

Now let's study Simon Peter's response to being in the presence of deity:

1One day as Jesus was standing by the Lake of Gennesaret, the people were crowding around him and listening to the word of God. 2He saw at the water's edge two boats, left there by the fishermen, who were washing their nets. 3He got into one of the boats, the one belonging to Simon, and

*asked him to put out a little from shore. Then he sat down
and taught the people from the boat.*

*⁴When he had finished speaking, he said to Simon, "Put out
into deep water, and let down the nets for a catch."*

*⁵Simon answered, "Master, we've worked hard all night and
haven't caught anything. But because you say so, I will let
down the nets."*

*⁶When they had done so, they caught such a large number of
fish that their nets began to break. ⁷So they signaled their
partners in the other boat to come and help them, and they
came and filled both boats so full that they began to sink.*

*⁸When Simon Peter saw this, he fell at Jesus' knees and
said, "Go away from me, Lord; I am a sinful man!" ⁹For he
and all his companions were astonished at the catch of fish
they had taken, ¹⁰and so were James and John, the sons of
Zebedee, Simon's partners.*

*Then Jesus said to Simon, "Don't be afraid; from now on you
will fish for people." ¹¹So they pulled their boats up on shore,
left everything and followed him* (Luke 5:1-11).

Perhaps the most important part of Simon's response is the
ending. Simon was never the same because he "left everything
and followed Him." This sentence speaks of a turning point in a
person's life when he encounters, realizes, and properly responds
to God's presence. We will focus more on life transformation in
chapter 5.

For further study, consider the call of Jeremiah. Read Jeremiah
1:1 thru 2:2.

Let's reflect on and consider the previously mentioned biblical examples of men of faith encountering God and realizing His presence as case studies for learning.

Realization

Focus on these case studies for a moment. What did it take in each story for the main character to come to a realization of God's presence?

With Jacob, it was a dream while he was on a journey. For Samuel, it was hearing the audible voice of God. Isaiah saw God in a vision and was sure he was going to die. Simon Peter witnessed a miracle performed by Jesus himself.

What will it take for you to come to the realization that we are in the presence of God?

Also, read what the Apostle Paul told the Athenians in Acts 17:22-28.

Brother Lawrence said, "He is nearer to us than we are aware of. It is not necessary ... to be at church [to be in His presence]. Everyone is capable of such familiar conversation with God .... Let us live and die with God [continually in His Presence]."[24]

Response

Of the previously mentioned biblical case studies in this chapter, to which one do you relate?

Based on our biblical case studies, what can we learn? What is the Holy Spirit trying to teach us about the proper response to God's presence? What do you think is the message we should receive?

Devotional Scripture

I believe the most inspiring scripture regarding the realization of God's presence is Psalm 139. This passage uses beautiful language to describe how God is all-powerful, all-knowing, and always present. Read and focus on the following passage from Psalm 139 and let the Holy Spirit speak to you through the living Word:

> *7Where can I go from your Spirit? Where can I flee from your presence?*
>
> *8If I go up to the heavens, you are there; if I make my bed in the depths, you are there.*
>
> *9If I rise on the wings of the dawn, if I settle on the far side of the sea, 10even there your hand will guide me, your right hand will hold me fast.*
>
> *11If I say, "Surely the darkness will hide me and the light become night around me," 12even the darkness will not be dark to you; the night will shine like the day, for darkness is as light to you.*
>
> *13For you created my inmost being; you knit me together in my mother's womb.*
>
> *14I praise you because I am fearfully and wonderfully made; your works are wonderful, I know that full well*
> (Psalm 139:7-14).

This passage praises and celebrates the fact that God's presence is everywhere. Worship should be our response to such a wonderful realization. We will focus more on this passage in chapter 9.

Application/Implication

The application and implication of God's presence is very straightforward and obvious from what we have already read. If you realize and believe we live in the presence of a loving and all-powerful God, then what should your response be? Do you believe these passages? Do you believe that God is a loving Father who watches over His children? Dwell on this knowledge for a few moments and then ask yourself, "How does this apply to me? How am I going to live differently?"

Life-Change Challenge:

Our challenge comes from the words of Brother Lawrence. Who is he?

Brother Lawrence was born Nicolas Herman and lived 1614–1691. He was uneducated and worked for a time as a soldier. He entered a monastery near Paris, France as a layman and worked in the kitchens and as a cobbler there for the remainder of his life. Brother Lawrence was like the "everyman" or unlikely hero of his peers. I'm not trying to disrespect or make light of this great man of faith. Just as we seem to gravitate to fictional characters that seem average but turn out to be people of great character like Marty McFly from the movie "Back To The Future" or J. R. R. Tolkien's character Bilbo Baggins, Brother Lawrence was a man people admired and sought out.

Even though he was not highly educated and he never held a high-ranking office in the church, people of esteem came to him for common-sense advice regarding spiritual closeness to God. Lawrence is known for his devotion and ability to bring God into every aspect of his life. His classic Christian work *Practice of the Presence of God* details how to gain that constant and comforting connection to God. Readers have treasured this short and easy-to-read book for centuries because of Lawrence's honest advice and his obvious passion for spiritual matters.

He rejoiced in everyday tasks, prayed constantly, and was known around the monastery for his kindness and willingness to help others. Here is some guidance from Brother Lawrence's book, which is a compilation of personal correspondence cobbled together by his followers after his death:

> "... in the beginning of his [practice of the presence of God], he spent the hours appointed for private prayer in thinking of GOD, so as to convince his mind of, and to impress deeply upon his heart, the Divine existence ... and submission to [God] .... That by this short and sure method, he exercised himself in the knowledge and love of GOD, resolving to use his utmost endeavor to live in a continual sense of His Presence.[25]

> "Let us think often that our only business in this life is to please God .... Let us think of Him perpetually .... How can we pray to Him without being with Him? How can we be with Him but in thinking of Him often? [Make this a] holy habit .... You will tell me that I am always saying the same thing; it is true, for this is the best and easiest method I know."[26]

Ponder the fact that we are in God's presence **all the time — coram Deo**. How are we like Peter (Luke 5), wanting to distance ourselves from a holy God? How much are we like Jacob, wanting to bargain with God? Are we like Isaiah? Do we need to see visions or hear voices to believe the reality of His Presence? Or do we believe what the Word teaches us about God's attributes? Consider this passage from Hebrews:

> [12]*For the word of God is alive and active. Sharper than any double-edged sword, it penetrates even to dividing soul and spirit, joints and marrow; it judges the thoughts and*

attitudes of the heart. [13]Nothing in all creation is hidden from God's sight. Everything is uncovered and laid bare before the eyes of him to whom we must give account (Hebrews 4:12-13).

These incredible statements boggle the mind. When we approach His throne in prayer, we should do so with **awe, reverence, and respect** (as the early church did) because we come before a holy and awesome God. This is an incredible privilege to have the ability to have an audience with God. Realizing such a right endowed by our Creator, we should pause and consider the gravity of enjoying such a blessing. **Keep praying.** Add another component to your daily prayer. When you start the prayer, actually say something like, "Dear Lord, as I **come before you** in this prayer." This may seem like a small thing but it is a reminder. Ask God to help you come to the full realization that you are continually in His presence and to make this practice a **holy habit** as Brother Lawrence advised. Let this realization change your whole perspective.

Consider also II Timothy 4:1-2 where Paul gives his final charge to his disciple Timothy:

[1]In the presence of God and of Christ Jesus, who will judge the living and the dead, and in view of his appearing and his kingdom, I give you this charge: [2]Preach the word; be prepared in season and out of season; correct, rebuke and encourage — with great patience and careful instruction (II Timothy 4:1-2).

Notice that Paul invokes the phrase, "in the presence of God" as a way of emphasizing the importance of the challenge. This is significant and had meaning to both the Apostle Paul as well as his student Timothy.

I would like to borrow from Paul and say to you, "in the presence of God" please take seriously the reality of the discipline we are learning that we are calling coram Deo. Take the advice of Brother Lawrence. **Think of God "perpetually."** Pray for God to give you a humble spirit, like Samuel, Simon Peter, and Isaiah. Our business in this life is to please God and to do His will. Make coram Deo your **holy habit.**

Looking Forward

In chapter 4, we are going to discuss the idea of "God-forsaken" times in our lives. Before we go any deeper into the disciplines of coram Deo, we need to bandage some wounds and reset expectations.

Now that we see God's loving plan for our lives and how He wants a close relationship with us, we can address the problem of sin and spiritual hiding as well as feeling distant from God. With our perspective clearly rooted in the knowledge of His plan and His omnipresence, we have to tackle that difficult riddle: If we are in God's presence all the time then why, at times, does it feel like we are all alone in our struggles? This is an area where many of us need frank discussion, some emotional and spiritual healing, and godly counsel. I pray that you will continue on this journey with me.

Chapter 4: God-Forsaken Times

Introduction

It is fair to say that the vast majority of people who have lived in this world to the age of adulthood have experienced what some would say are **desert** times, those times when we felt isolated, neglected, mistreated, as if we someone dealt us an unfair hand. In these times, we often feel separated from God. For the sake of this discussion, we will call these times the *God-forsaken* times. These are the points in our life when we might ask God, "Are you there? Is this how I deserve to be treated? What did I do to cause this? Are you punishing me? Why me, God?"

The purpose for this chapter is not necessarily to explain every possible reason for these times or to convince you that God is present despite our circumstances or feelings. The goal of this chapter is to help us

- be prepared for,

- cope with, and

- heal from the God-forsaken times, which will inevitably come.

Jesus tried to set the expectations of His disciples when He warned, "*I have told you these things, so that in me you may have peace. In this world you will have trouble. But take heart! I have overcome the world*" (John 16:33).

This chapter is designed to help reset our expectations as disciples and heal us from wounds we may have from God-forsaken times.

Have you experienced a God-forsaken time in your life? Most of us have.

Bible Study

God wants us to obey His Word and live moral, upstanding lives that will serve as examples to those outside the Body of Christ. When they see Christ in us through our good example, they will want to imitate us as the disciples of Christ imitated Him. If we live like this, God will always bless us and prosper us with the "abundant life" as we see in passages such as Psalm 1:1-3 and John 10:10.

Is there anything wrong with this logic?

There is certainly some truth there. But if someone believed this simplistic train of logic, thinking it to be the hard-and-fast rule, and thought that following God would **always** bless and prosper Christians, how would he or she explain when good Christian families experience painful cancer, debilitating heart disease, senseless violent crime, sudden infant death syndrome, lay-offs, depression, discouragement, bankruptcy, and all forms of human suffering?

The Christian life is just not that simple. It is not as easy as Repent>Follow God>Prosper (1>2>3). Dr. James Dobson wrote, "Clearly, the Scriptures tell us that we lack the capacity to grasp God's infinite mind or the way He intervenes in our lives. How arrogant of us to think otherwise! Trying to analyze His omnipotence is like an amoeba attempting to comprehend the behavior of a man."[27] Dobson references the following two Bible passages:

Oh, the depth of the riches of the wisdom and knowledge of God!

How unsearchable his judgments,

and his paths beyond tracing out! (Romans 11:33).

for, "Who has known the mind of the Lord so as to instruct him?"

But we have the mind of Christ (I Corinthians 2:16).

Dobson explains that the majority of us, perhaps even one hundred percent of believers, will someday feel alienated from God.[28] He references Job, the most righteous man of his day. Job was "blameless," yet sudden disaster fell on him. Even though Job did not sin during this trial, he did reach the point of **despair** when God hid His **presence** from view and the circumstances did not make sense. In this book, Dobson sites many faithful men and women (ancient and modern) who suffered greatly.

Great men of faith in our modern times have suffered great difficulties. C.S. Lewis wrote of his great pain and bewilderment after the death of his beloved wife. "Where is God? Go to Him when your need is desperate, when all other help is vain and what do you find? A door slammed in your face and a sound of bolting and double bolting on the inside. After that, silence."[29]

Rich Mullins wrote lyrics that conveyed the same sentiment. In the lyrics to the song entitled "Hard to Get" Rich is saying that God is hard to get.[30] This has a double meaning: That God is hard to understand but also meaning that it is hard to feel close to God. Mullins was just being honest about his feelings. This is a biblical concept. Consider the following Bible passages:

¹Why, Lord, do you stand far off? Why do you hide yourself in times of trouble?

²In his arrogance the wicked man hunts down the weak, who are caught in the schemes he devises.

³He boasts about the cravings of his heart; he blesses the greedy and reviles the Lord.

⁴In his pride the wicked man does not seek him; in all his thoughts there is no room for God.

⁵His ways are always prosperous; your laws are rejected by him; he sneers at all his enemies.

⁶He says to himself, "Nothing will ever shake me." He swears, "No one will ever do me harm" (Psalm 10:1-6).

How long, Lord? Will you forget me forever? How long will you hide your face from me? (Psalm 13:1).

⁷Will the Lord reject forever? Will he never show his favor again? ⁸Has his unfailing love vanished forever? Has his promise failed for all time? (Psalm 77:7-8).

¹Faith means being sure of the things we hope for and knowing that something is real even if we do not see it. ²Faith is the reason we remember great people who lived in the past.

³It is by faith we understand that the whole world was made by God's command so what we see was made by something that cannot be seen.

⁴It was by faith that Abel offered God a better sacrifice than Cain did. God said he was pleased with the gifts Abel offered and called Abel a good man because of his faith. Abel died, but through his faith he is still speaking.

56

⁵It was by faith that Enoch was taken to heaven so he would not die. He could not be found, because God had taken him away. Before he was taken, the Scripture says that he was a man who truly pleased God. ⁶Without faith no one can please God. Anyone who comes to God must believe that he is real and that he rewards those who truly want to find him.

⁷It was by faith that Noah heard God's warnings about things he could not yet see. He obeyed God and built a large boat to save his family. By his faith, Noah showed that the world was wrong, and he became one of those who are made right with God through faith (Hebrews 11:1-7 NCV).

Studying these biblical stories and understanding the foundation of faith and hope can teach us this vital principle from Dr. James Dobson: The Lord Can Be **Trusted** Even When He Can't Be **Tracked** (emphasis mine).[31]

Dwell on that simple statement for a moment. Let it sink in and bury it deep in your heart. If you get nothing else out of this chapter than full acceptance of that statement, then I will be satisfied that this chapter was a success.

As mentioned earlier, at some point in the lives of most men and women of faith we go through one of those deep valleys, those God-forsaken periods where we feel God has forgotten us or even mistreated us. Our faith and biblical knowledge tell us that God is omnipotent, omniscient, and omnipresent. He certainly could help me. We may think, "What have I done to deserve this abandonment? Haven't I served Him with a willing heart?'" Ultimately, confusion leads to frustration, which leads to distrust and bitterness.[32]

I have personally struggled with what Winston Churchill called "Black Dog" depression.[33] Several occasions in my life, I've gone through dark times when I felt like a failure and thought God had let me down. Most recently, I experienced a bout of depression shortly after a triumph in my life.

After graduating with a bachelor's degree and being out of college for 17 years, I decided to go back to college to obtain a Master's degree. I'm a glutton for punishment, right? The goal was to advance my career as a professional trainer in the information technology industry.

Following much hard work and effort, I graduated in 2009 expecting that this degree would open doors for me. However, nothing happened: no promotion, no raise, nothing. After about nine months, an overwhelming feeling of failure came over me. Had I wasted all of that time and effort? Was it for nothing that I sacrificed being away from my family, completing all of the voluminous reading and endless writing of papers? I knew this should not be enough to cause this kind of depression, but I could not shake it.

I tried to find another job, putting my updated resume on numerous career sites and working my professional network of contacts. All I got was more rejection. As you might expect, I got more and more depressed. During this time, it was hard to get out of bed and go to work. I was not motivated and could not seem to shake that feeling of worthlessness. I had hit a wall, and so I asked God, "Please show me the way because I hate where I am. I just want to do Your will, but I am miserable in my career."

Dobson describes this by saying, "[We] lose God. Doubt rises up to obscure His presence and disillusionment settles into **despair**" (emphasis mine).[34]

When this happens, the next step is what Dobson calls, "The Betrayal Barrier." The person of faith actually feels betrayed by God. This is a dangerous predicament for a child of God: resenting and feeling betrayed by God. Dobson says, "We must brace our brothers and sisters against the **betrayal barrier**" (emphasis mine)."[35]

John Ortberg made a similar statement: "We need a way of holding on to God when it feels as if God has let go of us."[36]

Borrowing a little from Dobson, Ortberg, and other writers, here is my own personal take on dealing with the betrayal barrier in our God-forsaken times:

The first step in bracing against the betrayal barrier is to **adjust our expectations**. We must realize that the scriptures teach us that trials and suffering are part of the human condition. Becoming a Christian and living a faithful life does not inoculate us from suffering. In fact, it might put us on Satan's hit list as we see with Job.

Remember the scripture mentioned earlier. It is worth reading again. Jesus told his disciples, *"I have told you these things, so that in me you may have peace. In this world you will have trouble. But take heart! I have overcome the world'* (John 16:33).

Consider what the Apostle Paul wrote to the church in Corinth:

> *4I have spoken to you with great frankness; I take great pride in you. I am greatly encouraged; in all our troubles my joy knows no bounds.*

> *5For when we came into Macedonia, we had no rest, but we were harassed at every turn — conflicts on the outside, fears within* (II Corinthians 7:4-5).

Do you see the strange duality that Paul is expressing? He was harassed at every turn with conflicts on the outside and fears within. Yet Paul still says, *"In all our troubles my joy knows no bounds."*

The Apostle Peter expresses the same theme:

12Dear friends, do not be surprised at the fiery ordeal that has come on you to test you, as though something strange were happening to you. 13But rejoice inasmuch as you participate in the sufferings of Christ, so that you may be overjoyed when his glory is revealed (I Peter 4:12-13).

As part of adjusting our expectations, another lesson we can learn from understanding the story of Job is to consider the upper and lower story perspectives in human history. The upper story is God's grand design and how He is sovereign (all powerful). Randy Frazee explains, "There is the Upper Story. God is real, He is present, and He is working on our behalf. Heaven is breaking into the world more than we recognize, and the story of God's seeking love, perpetual grace and longing for relationship with ordinary people is breathtaking."[37]

His will gets done one way or another, and we are often not grasping the upper story as life events unfold.

Then there is the lower story. This is life from our perspective. Frazee says, "We make mistakes, run from God, and resist his overtures of love. Sometimes we get so mired in the lower story that we fail to recognize God's presence breaking into our world."[38]

If we just look at the immediate circumstances going on around us, the feeling that life is out of control easily overwhelms us.

One of the central themes of Dr. Dobson's book is that we may never understand why things happen the way they do in this life. In the story of Job, he never was privy to the upper story, yet Job still had faith in God.

The second step in dealing with the betrayal barrier is understanding what the Lord calls us to do, which is to **learn how joy and pain can coexist.**

Consider these scriptures:

> *⁴Rejoice in the Lord always. I will say it again: Rejoice! ⁵Let your gentleness be evident to all. The Lord is near. ⁶Do not be anxious about anything, but in every situation, by prayer and petition, with thanksgiving, present your requests to God. ⁷And the peace of God, which transcends all understanding, will guard your hearts and your minds in Christ Jesus* (Philippians 4:4-7).

> *¹James, a servant of God and of the Lord Jesus Christ, To the twelve tribes scattered among the nations: Greetings. ²Consider it pure joy, my brothers and sisters, whenever you face trials of many kinds, ³because you know that the testing of your faith produces perseverance. ⁴Let perseverance finish its work so that you may be mature and complete, not lacking anything* (James 1:1-4).

"Jesus, like Job, was known as a man of sorrow. He himself would go through the winter of the absence of God: 'My God, my God, why have you forsaken me?'"[39]

Brother Lawrence said, "I have ... often [suffered] near [to the point of] expiring ... but I prayed for strength to suffer with courage, humility and love. Ah, how sweet is it to suffer with God!"[40]

Read that last sentence from Brother Lawrence again. That is the attitude we need to develop, the idea that it is a privilege and joy to suffer with God because He is with us every step of the way. We must learn that joy can coexist with suffering as part of our method of combating the betrayal barrier.

Third, we must **believe that God is present and involved in our lives** even when He seems absent. This relates directly with the theme of this entire study: We are in the constant presence of

God — coram Deo. Yet, in our lower story lives, we still experience what we think are God-forsaken times.

Consider these scriptures:

> ¹⁹*Therefore go and make disciples of all nations, baptizing them in the name of the Father and of the Son and of the Holy Spirit,* ²⁰*and teaching them to obey everything I have commanded you. And surely **I am with you always**, to the very end of the age* (Matthew 28:19-20, emphasis mine).

Our focus is often on the first part of this scripture as the Great Commission. However, also consider how important that last part is to us: *"I am with you always."*

> *For the eyes of the Lord are on the righteous and his ears are attentive to their prayer, but the face of the Lord is against those who do evil"* (I Peter 3:12).

Although it feels like God is absent, He is there. His eyes are on us and He is going to carry us through in the end.

Fourth, **God's timing is perfect**, even when He appears to be catastrophically late.

In John 11, we see an example of when God's timing initially seems way off. In this passage, Jesus receives word that a friend, Lazarus, is very sick. Rather than immediately stopping what He was doing and going to Lazarus to heal him, Jesus purposefully delays for two days. During that time, Lazarus dies, which leaves his sisters distraught and in a state of bewilderment, because they know that Jesus can heal the sick.

Jesus could have saved Lazareth. Jesus shows up a couple of days late and performs a miracle by raising Lazarus from the dead. By conventional wisdom, Jesus was late because He didn't drop everything and come to heal. But the Son of God's timing is perfect because He shows the world that He is not just the Great Physician but also the all-powerful source of life itself.

This is such an incredible lesson for us today. If God seems to be delaying answering a prayer the way you expect, then there is a reason. Either He is saying, "No" (because it is for our own good) or delaying for a reason. It is not that He doesn't love you or is punishing you. Quite the opposite. He knows best and the sooner we realize that God's timing is perfect and His will is best for us, the sooner we will heal from our perceived God-forsaken times. This is a lesson that I personally have to learn and relearn in my walk. It is not easy.

Brother Lawrence wrote:

> "I do not pray that you may be delivered from your pains, but I pray ... that He would give you strength and patience to bear them as long as He pleases. I wish you could convince yourself that God is often (in some sense) nearer to us and more effectually present with us, in sickness than in health.... Continue then always with God; 'tis the only support and comfort for your affliction" (emphasis mine)."[41]

This leads to our final step we should take to fight the betrayal barrier.

Last of all, Dobson says, "For reasons that are **impossible** to explain, **we human beings are incredibly precious to God**" (emphasis mine).[42]

> [17]*"What is mankind that you make so much of them, that you give them so much attention, [18]that you examine them every morning and test them every moment?* (Job 7:17-18).
>
> *What is mankind that you are mindful of them, human beings that you care for them?* (Psalm 8:4).

¹You have searched me, Lord, and you know me. ²You know when I sit and when I rise; you perceive my thoughts from afar. ³You discern my going out and my lying down; you are familiar with all my ways. ⁴Before a word is on my tongue you, Lord, know it completely (Psalm 139:1-4).

These are inspiring Scriptures given to remind and encourage us that God loves us **very** much. He is our heavenly Father and He knows what is best for us. It doesn't make sense that the Creator of the universe would care about our lower stories. But the fact is Jesus loves us. This I know, for the Bible tells us so.

Also consider these Scriptures: Luke 11:13; Psalm 103:13; Isaiah 66:13; John 3:16.

Dobson tells us:

> "If we truly understood the majesty" of our Lord and His fathomless love for us "we would certainly accept those times when He defies human logic …. [We must] expect confusing experiences to occur along the way. Welcome them … as opportunities for your faith to grow. Hold fast to your faith, without which it is impossible to please Him. Never let yourself succumb to the 'betrayal barrier', which is [one of] Satan's … [most] effective tools against us. Instead, store away your questions for a lengthy conversation on the other side [with our loving Father in heaven]."⁴³

The only thing that pulled me through my Black Dog depression was my Lord, my faith, and my family. My career expectations may never be realized, but I can rest in the knowledge that my Father loves me, my family loves me, and I have the privilege to serve in a Kingdom that has no bounds. When I get the right upper story perspective, then office politics, professional titles, and window offices begin to look petty.

Brother Lawrence expressed it like this:

"If we knew how much He loves us, we should be always ready to receive equally and with indifference from His hand the sweet and the bitter; all would please that came from Him .... When we see them [the sorest afflictions] in the hand of God ... when we know that it is [from] our loving Father ... our sufferings will lose their bitterness."[44]

For more in-depth study, consider reading the entire book of Job and Hebrews chapter 11.

Satan's point of argument in the story of Job is that human beings are not capable of true faith and true dedication; they are in it for themselves for selfish reasons. Ortberg explains, "The question is, 'can a human being hold on to God in the face of suffering?' Notice what Job says, 'Shall we accept good from God and not trouble?'"[45]

Consider the behavior of various heroes of the faith listed in Hebrews 11. Look closely at the behavior and actions of each person. Think about how each believer acted in faith. Did their story prove or disprove Satan's point of argument? Were they following God for their own personal gain? I would argue they were living out true faith in the face of hardship.

Devotional Scripture

Now let's pause for a moment and focus on a couple of scriptures, devoting our full attention to the Word of God.

> [17]*Blessed is the one whom God corrects; so do not despise the discipline of the Almighty.* [18]*For he wounds, but he also binds up; he injures, but his hands also heal* (Job 5:17-18).

> [15]*Though he slay me, yet will I hope in him; I will surely defend my ways to his face.* [16]*Indeed, this will turn out for*

my deliverance, for no godless person would dare come before him! (Job 13:15-16).

These two passages from Job speak to the fact that sometimes it appears God wounds us or slays us. In times like this, we must lean on our faith in Him and know that in the end, if we trust Him, it will turn out for our deliverance. The analogy that comes to mind is a young child going to the doctor. The child may feel betrayed by his or her parents at being delivered into the hands of a mean doctor who inflicts pain. Nevertheless, even if the doctor hurts the child with a shot or the painful realignment of a broken bone, a mature understanding of the bigger picture reveals that parents and the doctor are doing it for the good of the child.

Application/Implication

The epistle of James actually says that trials and testing are for our good (James 1:2-4, 12). It says that difficulties develop perseverance and make us more mature. Paul also said in Romans 8:28 that God works for our good in all situations.

Another analogy comes to mind. How do you build strength in your muscles and respiratory system? It might seem counterintuitive on the surface that we build our muscles up by tearing them down aggressively through vigorous exercise that completely exhausts the body and pushes it to the limit. There is some truth in the common saying "no pain, no gain." This is also true of our spiritual fitness. As most people understand through their own experiences, our faith typically grows most during testing and pain just as our muscles grow from vigorous exercise and strain.

One additional point Ortberg discusses regarding enduring difficult and painful times is that in a way God is telling us, "I'm worth it. Life, following me — it's all worth it. Don't give up. The pain is not going to last forever. I am the kind of God who is worth getting close to."[46]

This is a biblical concept. The Apostle Paul, a true authority on suffering because of his faith, wrote to the Roman church and said, *"I consider that our present sufferings are not worth comparing with the glory that will be revealed in us"* (Romans 8:18).

Our present suffering will not compare to the wonderful reward we will receive in eternity with our Lord. We simply have to trust Him and endure. That is faith. We need to understand bad things happen to good people and good things happen to bad people. This is another example of expectations and human perspective. In God's eyes, we are all sinful people, yet He allows the rain to fall on the righteous and the unrighteous. The truth is none of us is truly "righteous" in the presence of our holy, holy, holy God.

How can we better cope with the God-forsaken times in our lives?

Life-Change Challenge

Based on this chapter, please reflect on the five steps mentioned earlier about bracing against the **betrayal barrier**. Are you currently experiencing a God-forsaken desert time in your life? Do you know someone dealing with a desert time in his or her life? If so, spend some time this week praying about the situation and asking for God's help.

Brother Lawrence wrote to encourage and to challenge a colleague going through a difficult time, "Ask of God, not deliverance from your pains, but strength to bear resolutely, for the love of Him, all that He should please, and as long as He shall please."[47]

That is a proper perspective on suffering.

Brother Lawrence also wrote:

> "Take courage; offer Him your pains incessantly, pray to Him for strength to endure them .... Adore Him in your infirmities, offer yourself to Him ... and in the height of your sufferings, beseech Him humbly and affectionately (as a child his father) to make you [not comfortable, but] conformable to [His] holy will."[48]

Here is the real life-change challenge: Think back on a time in your life when you struggled and felt betrayed or abandoned by God. I'm going to ask you to do something that you may consider odd. Please **reevaluate** that time in your life in view of this discussion. View it through a new lens, with the full knowledge that God is a loving father that would not have allowed you to suffer for no reason. Reflect on that God-forsaken time and pray for God to help you see it as a time of growth for your faith and your witness.

For me, I had to rethink my Master's degree and trust that God is using that investment of time and sacrifice for His work. The privilege to do His work is better than a career opportunity. I believe my Master's degree produced tangible positive results in my professional career in Information Technology, even though it was not rewarded. However, I trust that this experience has made me a better teacher and servant of the church, which is even more valuable.

It is not easy or natural to rewrite a memory and see it in a new light. It may help to have a role model. Consider the story of Joseph. We don't have a detailed journal of his feelings, but perhaps he is someone who had to reconsider his own plight. Remember what he endured: thrown in a pit by his jealous brothers, sold into slavery, mistreated, slandered by Potiphar's wife, and thrown into prison. It would have been easy for Joseph to have a pity party or to feel betrayed by God, but we don't see that happening in the Bible story. Instead, Joseph sees the upper story rather than wallowing in the unfairness of the lower story.

When Joseph revealed himself to his brothers, he said, "But God sent me ahead of you to preserve for you a remnant on earth and to save your lives by a great deliverance" (Genesis 45:7). He overcame the betrayal barrier.

Another role model who overcame a significant lower story problem is Esther. She and all Jews in her country were about to be slaughtered. Moreover, Mordecai, her relative, warned her that this difficult time was not the time to shrink back in fear or inaction. Instead, he encouraged Esther and said to her, "Who knows but that you have come to royal position for such a time as this" (Esther 4:14).

God had engineered circumstances in just the right way for Esther to endure this desert moment and rise to the occasion. Her response to the peril of her people was about to become her legacy. God is **the great circumstance engineer**.

My favorite passage in the entire Bible is Romans 8:28.

> *And we know that in all things God works for the good of those who love Him and who are called according to His purpose* (Romans 8:28).

Who is doing the work in this passage? It says, "**GOD** works." This is about His divine providence and His upper story. We may not understand what He is doing. Job never understood what was going on in the upper story. Nevertheless, he managed to trust God through his lower story catastrophe and **never** cursed God, nor did he sin in those difficult circumstances.

Can we do the same? Do we have that kind of faith? We all need to pray for that kind of faith. We all need to pray for the vision and understanding that Joseph, Esther, and Mordecai exhibited. We need the faith and endurance of Job. Let these men and women of faith instruct and inspire you. Rewrite your own desert times and **know** that during that time, God was working for your good. No experience is wasted because each is part of God's grand scheme to prepare us to serve in this life and to worship Him in the next life.

God can be **trusted**, even if our feeble mind is not able to **track** the logic of His ways. In your mind, rewrite your desert time and realize it was not an example of being "forsaken" by God, but rather a God-ordained time of testing and faith building. Use the fact that your faith survived those struggles as a witness to God's providence and protection (ref: I Cor. 10:13).

Look for ways to use the struggle you endured to help someone else who is struggling. Let this line of thinking challenge you. Keep up your daily prayers. Keep seeking God. As you remove the barriers in your life that stand between you and Him, keep practicing the holy habit of **coram Deo**, and living in His presence **constantly**.

Looking Forward

So far we have discussed God's design for mankind through a personal relationship with us (chapter 1), and the value of seeking God rather than hiding from Him (chapter 2). We also studied the proper response to the realization of His presence (chapter 3) and bracing against the betrayal barrier (chapter 4).

Next, we will talk about renewing our minds. We will use the alliteration of head, heart, and habits. First, we must understand God's presence, learning coram Deo, getting it in our heads (chapter 5). Then, we need to get coram Deo in our hearts (chapter 6 on transformation). After we have embraced God's presence in our head and heart, then our habits will follow (chapter 7).

Chapter 5: Renewing Our Minds

Introduction

In this chapter, we discuss renewing our minds in the context of coram Deo by briefly studying Martin Luther's statements about conscience. We will also discuss how the power of God renews our minds.

This study had its genesis in my mind from a few lines written in Charles Colson's book *The Body* that explained the Latin phrase coram Deo. Colson writes:

> "During the Reformation, Coram Deo became a rallying cry for the Reformers. It meant 'in the presence of' or 'before the eyes of God' .... It drove the Reformers to their knees in fear and reverence. [Colson describes how the early church was filled with awe and holy fear of God]. How desperately the church today needs to take hold of that awe! To understand that we live day by day in the presence of God ... Coram Deo. Filled with this holy fear and reverence, the early church changed the world and the Reformers transformed the church and the culture."[49]

> "Seized by this biblically informed view of life ... Filled with the fear of God — the deepest reverence of the Lord Almighty — their cry became Coram Deo, 'in the presence of God.' And nothing could stop them. [The Reformation changed history]."[50]

73

Born in Germany in 1483, Martin Luther became one of the most influential figures in Christian history when he began the Protestant Reformation in the 16th century. He called into question some of the basic tenets of Roman Catholicism, and his followers soon split from the Roman Catholic Church to begin the Protestant tradition.[51]

His most significant act was posting a grievance list of Ninety-five Theses on a church door in Wittenberg, Germany. It was a huge milestone in human history and was an indictment against church corruption. Following that action, Luther was put on trial at The Diet of Worms. Luther was asked to recant. Instead, Luther gave his famous "Here I Stand" speech. In that speech, Luther said:

> "I am bound by the Scriptures I have quoted. **My conscience is captive to the Word of God.** I cannot and will not retract anything, for to go against conscience is neither right nor safe. God help me. Amen" (emphasis mine).[52]

Luther, of course, did not recant and did not put aside his conscience. He acted in accordance with his Bible knowledge and his conscience. By doing so, he revealed his understanding of coram Deo. Luther's writings indicate that he based his understanding of conscience on the conviction that human beings exist coram Deo. The reformer was convinced that all of life is lived and judged by conscience "before God."

A few months after the Diet of Worms, Luther summarized his insight about conscience and coram Deo.

> "Conscience is not the power to do works, but to judge them. The proper work of conscience, as Paul says in Romans 2:15, is to accuse or excuse, to make guilty or guiltless ... this judgment makes us stand accused or saved in God's sight; coram Deo."[53]

Lutheran commentators explain it like this. "Luther bases his understanding of conscience on the conviction that human beings exist: 'coram Deo,' in Latin [it means] 'in the sight of God.'"[54]

Bible Study

How can we have minds that are receptive to God's presence? Kent Hughes says, "Brothers, as Christians we are free to have a Christian mind. It is within our reach, and it is our duty."[55]

> *2I will be careful to lead a blameless life — when will you come to me?*
>
> *I will conduct the affairs of my house with a blameless heart.*
>
> *3I will not look with approval on anything that is vile.*
>
> *I hate what faithless people do; I will have no part in it* (Psalm 101, 2-3).

The first step for us is to **change our mindset**. We need to recognize that mankind's thinking is flawed. It is counter to God's will. We must think differently from the world. Our challenge is to **reject** the prevailing thought pattern of the world that is **me-centered** and does not take God and His plan into consideration. It is a **counterfeit** set of values, good in the mind of men, but actually opposed to God and often vile. The Apostle Paul said it like this.

> *21For although they knew God, they neither glorified him as God nor gave thanks to him, but their thinking became futile and their foolish hearts were darkened. 22Although they claimed to be wise, they became fools 23and exchanged the glory of the immortal God for images made to look like a mortal human being and birds and animals and reptiles.*

24Therefore God gave them over in the sinful desires of their hearts to sexual impurity for the degrading of their bodies with one another. 25They exchanged the truth about God for a lie, and worshiped and served created things rather than the Creator — who is forever praised. Amen (Romans 1:21-25).

A very common illustration about understanding the genuine article versus a counterfeit comes from a real life-training situation. Federal agents don't learn to spot counterfeit money by studying the counterfeits. They study genuine bills until they master the look of the real thing. Then when they see the bogus money, they recognize it. This is an often-quoted illustration in several places including John MacArthur's book *Reckless Faith*.56 It turns out that John MacArthur is correct. Training in identifying counterfeit currency means primarily studying the genuine article and spending very little time looking at the fake money.

As Christians, we need to be trained primarily on understanding God's perspective. Then, as we live our lives in this misguided world, we will be able to spot godly thinking as opposed to carnal counterfeits.

In this fallen world, there are pressures to blend in and be like the rest of our society. It is easier to just fit in and be molded into the image of the pop culture of the day. But God's Word advises a different approach.

Do not be conformed to this world (this age), [fashioned after and adapted to its external, superficial customs], but be transformed (changed) by the [entire] renewal of your mind [by its new ideals and its new attitude], so that you may prove [for yourselves] what is the good and acceptable and perfect will of God, even the thing which is good and acceptable and perfect [in His sight for you] (Romans 12:2 AMP).

If we do not resist the world's paradigm, we could miss God's plan for our lives. Conforming to mankind's views will interfere with our ability to live coram Deo. The result of conforming to modern society is inviting God's wrath on us as Paul wrote to the Roman church. Reading the entire passage of Romans 1:18-32 is eye opening.

The opposite of cultivating a mind receptive to God is to ignore or reject God as this passage describes. It also repeats three times an ominous consequence of rejecting God and ignoring knowledge of Him: *"God gave them over to ...."* The phrase **gave over** is from the Greek word: *paradidómi*. Bible scholars say that this phrase "seems to have originated from the Jewish formulas of excommunication ... a person banished from the theocratic assembly was regarded as deprived of the protection of God."[57]

The result is that the person becomes a slave to his passions. Psalm 10:4 speaks about the wicked man and says, *"in all his thoughts there is no room for God."* How sad. Perhaps the verse with the strongest language on this topic is in the epistle of James:

> *You adulteresses, do you not know that friendship with the world is hostility toward God? Therefore whoever wishes to be a friend of the world makes himself an enemy of God* (James 4:4 NASB).

John Ortberg writes:

> "Make your mind the dwelling place of God. The goal here is to have a mind in which the glorious Father of Jesus is always present and gradually crowds out every distorted belief, every destructive feeling, and every misguided intention. [The result will be a mind dominated by] love, joy

and peace — three primary components of the fruit of the Spirit."[58]

Second, in addition to changing our mindset, we also need to **focus** our minds. Our mind is constantly flowing from one thing to the next. It is not easy to stay focused on God. The Apostle Paul gives us this advice:

[4]Rejoice in the Lord always. I will say it again: Rejoice!

[5]Let your gentleness be evident to all. The Lord is near. [6]Do not be anxious about anything, but in every situation, by prayer and petition, with thanksgiving, present your requests to God. [7]And the peace of God, which transcends all understanding, will guard your hearts and your minds in Christ Jesus. [8]Finally, brothers and sisters, whatever is true, whatever is noble, whatever is right, whatever is pure, whatever is lovely, whatever is admirable — if anything is excellent or praiseworthy — think about such things.

[9]Whatever you have learned or received or heard from me, or seen in me — put it into practice. And the God of peace will be with you (Philippians 4:4-9).

Again, we have the godly counsel of filling our minds with Spirit-directed thoughts that will push out anxiety and fill us with joy and peace. Colossians 3:2 echoes this concept when it says to set our minds on things above. These are some of the tenets of living coram Deo.

Sarah Young in her bestselling book *Jesus Calling* speaks to the need to focus our minds. Writing as if Jesus were speaking, she writes:

"Let me control your mind. The mind is the most restless, unruly part of mankind. Long after you have learned the discipline of holding your tongue, your thoughts defy your will and set themselves up against Me. ... I made you in My image, precariously close to deity. Though My blood has fully redeemed you, your mind is the last bastion of rebellion. Open yourself to My radiant Presence, letting My Light permeate your thinking. When My Spirit is controlling your mind, you are filled with Life and Peace."[59]

Third, Paul teaches us how we handle those times when our mind gets off track, those times when our thoughts of God are challenged and maybe even displaced by demonic forces that have **attacked** our minds.

> [3]For though we live in the world, we do not wage war as the world does. [4]The weapons we fight with are not the weapons of the world. On the contrary, they have divine power to demolish strongholds. [5]We demolish arguments and every pretension that sets itself up against the knowledge of God, and we take captive every thought to make it obedient to Christ. [6]And we will be ready to punish every act of disobedience, once your obedience is complete
> (II Corinthians 10:3-6).

The imagery in this passage is that of being at war. When you are at war, you have a certain heightened level of diligence, intensity, and intentionality.

Lastly, let's revisit the context of this chapter's focus passage.

> [1]Therefore, I urge you, brothers and sisters, in view of God's mercy, to offer your bodies as a living sacrifice, holy and pleasing to God — this is your true and proper worship. [2]Do not conform to the pattern of this world, but be transformed by the renewing of your mind. Then you will be able to test and approve what God's will is — his good, pleasing and perfect will (Romans 12:1-2).

Being transformed by the renewing of our minds is in the context of self-sacrifice. It does **not** say, "Transform yourself by your effort to control your thoughts and renew your mind." It implies that we are to "be transformed" and the way we will be transformed is by the renewing of our minds.

Who is doing the renewing? II Corinthians 5:17 says we are a new creature. This is the act of rebirth, being born again through the work of the Holy Spirit. When we surrender to God and make Jesus Lord and Savior of our life, the transformation begins as we become a new creation.

There are many passages on conscience that no doubt shaped Martin Luther's view of conscience. Here are just a few with a brief summary with each:

- In Genesis 20:1-7 Abimelech took Sarah as a wife with a clear conscience, not knowing she was married to Abraham.

- In I Samuel 24:1-6 David is "conscience-stricken" for cutting off a corner of King Saul's robe.

- In Acts 23:1 and 24:16 Paul acted in good conscience when he turned to faith in Jesus Christ.

- In I Corinthians 8 our conscience should convict us when we do things that could cause our brothers and sisters to stumble.

For additional study concerning the mind and conscience, read:

- Romans 2:15; 9:1

- I Corinthians 4:1-5; 8

- Ephesians 4:17- 5:21

- II Peter 3:18

- Phil. 3:12

- II Corinthians 3:18

Devotional Scripture

Now let's focus on a Bible passage for our devotional scripture. For a few moments, turn all of your attention on the following scripture:

> *16All Scripture is inspired by God and is useful to teach us what is true and to make us realize what is wrong in our lives. It corrects us when we are wrong and teaches us to do what is right. 17God uses it to prepare and equip his people to do every good work* (2 Timothy 3:16-17 NLT).

The passage is very detailed regarding the purpose of God's inspired Word. God's Word:

- is inspired by God;

- is useful to teach us truth;

- makes us realize what is wrong in our lives (ref: our discussion of counterfeits);

- corrects us (more than just realizing the wrong; it shows us how to correct the wrong);

- teaches us to do what is right (more than just what is right; it teaches us how to do it);

- and is used by God to prepare and equip His people to do every good work.

This understanding of the Scriptures is vital to renewing our minds, getting our heads filled with the living Word, and learning the discipline of coram Deo.

Application/Implication

Ponder these questions:

- What are some of the dominant thoughts in today's culture that are in opposition to God?

- What are some values mankind considers "good" that are contrary to biblical values?

In what areas do you think we (the church) need our minds renewed?

Tozer writes:

> "At the heart of the Christian message is God Himself waiting for His redeemed children to push in to **conscious awareness of His Presence**. ...The Universal Presence is a fact. God is here. The whole universe is alive with His life. And He is no strange or foreign God, but the familiar Father of our Lord Jesus Christ whose love has for these thousands of years enfolded the sinful race of men. And always He is trying to get our **attention**, to reveal Himself to us, to communicate with us. We have within us the ability to know Him if we will but respond to His overtures" (emphasis mine).[60]

So that raises the question of how. How can we "be transformed by the renewing of our minds?"

As stated earlier, we cannot do this solely by our own efforts. There is not a simple self-help exercise for us to do in order to complete the work of renewing our minds. I love how Tozer explains it as being on our journey to experience God's presence. He says, "There is no nice neat formula for this. Rather, we need to whet the spiritual appetite for that which it truly craves: the presence of God."[61] "Delighting in God's presence is not a do-it-yourself project."[62] Tozer explains that we need an experienced guide, our high priest, Jesus Christ.

God works on us, shaping our minds like a potter molding clay. Indeed II Timothy 1:7 says that God gives us not spirits of timidity but spirits of power and of love and **sound minds** (KJV). God gives us renewed minds and sound minds. The more we rely on God for renewing our minds and the less on our efforts, the better. In John 3:30, we see that John the Baptist had the right idea, more of Him and less of me. Earlier we looked at Colossian 3:2. Look at this verse in the context of renewing our minds.

> *[1]Since, then, you have been raised with Christ, set your hearts on things above, where Christ is, seated at the right hand of God. [2]Set your minds on things above, not on earthly things. [3]For you died, and your life is now hidden with Christ in God. [4]When Christ, who is your life, appears, then you also will appear with him in glory* (Colossians 3:1-4).

It literally says that when we accept Christ, we die to ourselves and He hides our lives in Him.

Just because we cannot transform ourselves or renew our own minds based on only our efforts does **not** mean we have no part in it. We have our parts in God's design. One of the best ways to do our part in renewing our minds is to fill our minds with Him. The most obvious method of filling our minds with God is to simply read and study His Word regularly.

Sadly, numerous studies over the years indicate that Christians do not read their Bibles regularly. I have heard many sermons and read multiple books that quote from polling sources such as Gallop and Barna that indicate only between ten and twenty percent of professing Christians claim they read the Bible regularly. Yet we know that living in our modern society means counterfeit messages bombard us from every side every day. The best way to counter that wave of untruth is to do our part to renew our minds by feeding on the Word of God daily. This is how we live coram Deo.

Our minds need knowledge of the Creator. Second Peter 3:17-18 says we need knowledge and wisdom. Knowledge about God is extremely important. However, knowing is not enough.

> *15Be very careful, then, how you live — not as unwise but as wise, 16making the most of every opportunity, because the days are evil. 17Therefore do not be foolish, but understand what the Lord's will is* (Ephesians 5:15-17).

> *Do not merely listen to the word, and so deceive yourselves. Do what it says* (James 1:22).

God calls us to be doers of the Word, not just hearers of the Word. But you have to hear it (read it) first before you can do it. If only ten percent of Christians are reading the Word regularly, then we need to step up our game. God has higher expectations of disciples of Christ. We need to live wisely. Another important Scripture goes so far as to say that as mature disciples of Christ we have *"the mind of Christ"* (I Corinthians 2:6-16).

The spiritual discipline that is our focus for this chapter is renewing our minds by feeding on the Word of God regularly. This means that we are choosing God rather than self; choosing to give our time to God, reading His Word, rather than to our own selfish agenda or our own will. At first, this will seem like a sacrifice; but over time, as the mind is renewed, we will learn to crave our quiet time with God.

C.S. Lewis expressed a view about our willingness to submit to God's will in the following quote: "There are only two kinds of people in the end: Those who say to God, 'Thy will be done,' and those to whom God says, in the end, 'Thy will be done.'"[63]

This quote is also sometimes paraphrased as, "There are two kinds of people: Those who say to God, 'Thy will be done,' and those to whom God says, 'All right, then, have it your way.'"[64]

Obviously, we need to be the kind of people who spend their lives saying to God, "Thy will be done," because our will is not perfect. His will for us is perfect. Our selfish agenda is flawed.

Specifically, how can we grow in the knowledge of Christ?

Reflect on the concepts presented in this chapter, and then ask yourself:

How can I make my mind more receptive to God's will and the truth?

What areas of my mind have been polluted by the world and need renewing with the inspired Word of God?

What strongholds do I face and thoughts do I struggle with where I need God's help to take captive and make them obedient to Christ? (Ref: II Cor. 10:4-5).

Brother Lawrence said, "And I make it my business only to persevere in His holy presence, wherein I keep myself by a simple attention."[65]

Life-Change Challenge

For this challenge, please reflect on the concept of renewing your mind and make an intentional plan to fill your mind with His Word daily. If you do not have a reading plan and you want one, there are numerous daily devotional books available in most bookstores and online daily reading plans on Christian websites. Some are even free on websites like www.biblegateway.com.

If you just want an easy place to start, consider reading a chapter a day of the Gospel of John in a modern translation like the New International Version. John is an easy-to-read, encouraging book of the Bible that will help you get started. Psalms and Proverbs are also good starting points.

Listen for God's leading as you go through your day-to-day routine. Ask yourself, "How can I allow God to transform my mindset, crowd out the counterfeit pop culture, and replace the bad thoughts with the genuine truths of God?" This is how you can continue the process of being a new creation in Christ.

In this way, you can begin to train yourself to be more Christ-like, allowing Him to renew your mind and transform you. It will draw you closer to our Father in the discipline of coram Deo.

Looking Forward

In the next chapter, we will look even deeper into the concept of spiritual transformation. Renewing our minds is part of laying the groundwork for this complete transformation, which includes both our heads and our hearts.

Chapter 6: Transformation

Introduction

A close encounter with God can and should completely **transform** your life. In this chapter, we will explore the transformation of Moses after he encountered God in the burning bush. Additionally, we will study the radical difference in Saul after his encounter with Christ on the road to Damascus.

Here are a few examples of lives that were transformed. Do you remember those elementary school exercises that asked you to identify "which one does not belong?" See if you can figure out this puzzle.

Person	Before	After
John Newton	Unruly sailor, slave-trader who spoke against the Christian faith	Saved from a ship-wreck, converted to Christianity, became a preacher, wrote the song "Amazing Grace"
Charles Colson	Soldier, lawyer, special counsel to President Nixon, known as "Nixon's hatchet man", pled guilty to crimes related to the "Watergate scandal," went to prison	During the Watergate trial, a close friend gave him a copy of *Mere Christianity* by C. S. Lewis; reading it led Colson to become an evangelical Christian. His midlife conversion sparked a **radical** life-change that led to the founding of his nonprofit ministry *Prison Fellowship*. He was also a best-selling author.

Josh McDowell	McDowell struggled with low self-esteem. His father was an abusive alcoholic. McDowell was a mechanic in the Air National Guard discharged due to injury. He intended to pursue legal studies and a political career. He was an agnostic. While attending Kellogg Community College, he intended to write a paper on the historical evidence of Christian faith in order to **disprove** it.	Because of the evidence he found during his research, he converted to Christianity. Then he pursued Christian education, culminating in Talbot Theological Seminary. He gained a Master of Divinity degree, graduating Magna Cum Laude. He is now a best-selling author, speaker, and leading Christian apologist.
Miley Cyrus	She was raised in a Christian home and baptized in a Southern Baptist church near Nashville. She attended church regularly while growing up and even wore a purity ring.	She moved to Hollywood in 2005 because of entertainment roles. Now she is well known for her provocative image that overshadows her Disney family roles.

Obviously, one of the examples above was a transformation in the opposite direction than the others. Maybe your life does not reflect a profound or obvious transformation like these figures, but it is true that as a Christian you are a new creation in Christ (II Corinthians 5:17). It is God's design for us to be transformed into the likeness of His Son (II Corinthians 3:17-18).

Bible Study

We often think of Moses as a towering figure of faith from the Holy Scriptures, but he was a man who went through a **transformation** after a close encounter with God. However, it did not happen overnight. The book of Exodus reveals that he was born into a time of great struggle while the Israelites were slaves and Pharaoh was slaughtering babies (Exodus 1:12 - 22). Pharaoh's daughter saved him and brought him up with full knowledge of his ancestry (Exodus 2:11). He had a heart for his people and even killed an Egyptian who was beating a Hebrew (Exodus 2:12-13). He spent forty years as a fugitive, tending flocks in the wilderness of Midian (Exodus 2:14-3:1). He was slow of speech and a very reluctant leader, trying to bargain with God, and not wanting to obey His direct commands (Exodus 3).

Here are a few key scriptures showing Moses before and after the transformation which resulted from his encounter and show his developing relationship with God:

	Before	After
Moses	**Moses murdered an Egyptian slave-master.** *Glancing this way and that and seeing no one, he killed the Egyptian and hid him in the sand* (Exodus 2:12). **Moses did not want to obey God and lead the people:** *But Moses said, "O Lord, please send someone else to do it* (Exodus 4:13). See also Exodus 6:28-7:2	**Moses obeyed God and did lead the people** *Moses and Aaron brought together all the elders of the Israelites ... And they believed. And when they heard that the Lord was concerned about them and had seen their misery, they bowed down and worshipped* (Exodus 4:29,31). *During the night Pharaoh summoned Moses and Aaron and said, "Up! Leave my people, you and the Israelites! Go, worship the Lord as you have requested. Take your flocks and herds, as you have said, and go. And also bless me"* (Exodus 12:31-32). *Moses answered the people, "Do not be afraid. Stand firm and you will see the deliverance the Lord will bring you today. The Egyptians you see today you will never see again. The Lord will fight for you; you need only to be still'* (Exodus 14:13-14).

In chapter one, we studied God's original plan for mankind which included a close relationship with God. We have described the mistakes of hiding or running from God and of thinking that God has abandoned us during our desert moments in life. We have also seen that we need to realize that we are in God's presence all the time.

As we read the story of Moses in the Scriptures, we see that he seems to grasp that God wants a close relationship with him. Over time, Moses submits to God's will, even though Moses was a reluctant leader at first. Moses had a true coram Deo or face-to-face relationship with God. They spoke like friends. Moses was transformed and enjoyed a unique, intimate relationship with God that is without parallel.

> *The Lord would speak to Moses face to face, as one speaks to a friend. Then Moses would return to the camp* (Exodus 33:11a).

> *Since then, no prophet has risen in Israel like Moses, whom the Lord knew face to face* (Deuteronomy 34:10).

Moses was not perfect. However, he was considered a "friend" of God. That term friend is the same term Jesus used in the last days before He was crucified. Jesus told the disciples they were no longer just servants but were His friends.

> *I no longer call you servants, because a servant does not know his master's business. Instead, I have called you friends, for everything that I learned from my Father I have made known to you* (John 15:15).

Exodus 34:29-35 says that Moses was literally transformed. The Israelites noticed that after Moses met with God on Mount Sinai, "he was not aware that his face was radiant." Being in God's presence will change us. To be clear, our faces will not actually illuminate as Moses' face did. However, as disciples of Christ, we are called to be different from the world.

Jesus calls us to be "a city on a hill" and "the light of the world" (Matthew 5). The truth is that our actions should be so divergent from the world that we stand out as a reflection of Christ. We may not glow like Moses, but we should act and behave so differently that people take note. Do people notice you are different? If so, glory to God. They are probably seeing the fruit of the Spirit in you.

Now let's consider another example of transformation, Saul who became known as Paul:

	"Before"	"After"
Saul > Paul	[The disciple Stephen was stoned to death and his killers] ... *laid their coats at the feet of a young man named Saul ... And Saul approved of their killing him. On that day a great persecution broke out against the church in Jerusalem, and all except the apostles were scattered throughout Judea and Samaria .... But Saul began to destroy the church. Going from house to house, he dragged off both men and women and put them in prison* (Acts 7:54-8:5). *Meanwhile, Saul was*	[After Saul encountered Jesus and was blinded on the road to Damascus] *Ananias went to the house and entered it. Placing his hands on Saul, he said, "Brother Saul, the Lord — Jesus, who appeared to you on the road as you were coming here — has sent me so that you may see again and be filled with the Holy Spirit." Immediately, something like scales fell from Saul's eyes, and he could see again. He got up and was baptized, and after taking some food, he regained his strength. Saul spent several days with the disciples in Damascus. At once he began to preach in the synagogues that Jesus is*

still breathing out murderous threats against the Lord's disciples. He went to the high priest and asked him for letters to the synagogues in Damascus, so that if he found any there who belonged to the Way, whether men or women, he might take them as prisoners to Jerusalem (Acts 9:1-2).	*the Son of God* (Acts 9:17-20). *Then Barnabas went to Tarsus to look for Saul, and when he found him, he brought him to Antioch. So for a whole year Barnabas and Saul met with the church and taught great numbers of people. The disciples were called Christians first at Antioch* (Acts 11:25-26).

These passages show a radical transformation in Saul. He went from persecuting the church and throwing Christians into prison to accepting Jesus Christ as his Lord and Savior and preaching the Word to great numbers of people. As we read through the rest of Acts (chapters 13-28), we see Saul's name is changed to Paul and he becomes one of the most important figures in the early church, serving as a missionary, church leader, apostle, and inspired writer of many books in our Bible.

For further study, consider the transformation of the eleven surviving apostles after Christ's resurrection. They were ordinary men from various backgrounds: Peter and Andrew were fishermen; Bartholomew may have come from a royal family; Matthew was a tax collector, an occupation considered treason by many Jews. In contrast, Simon the Zealot was fanatically loyal to the nation of Israel. They were not men of high education, great wealth, or prominent position. Yet through them, Christ established His church and God changed the world.

Moreover, the people of their day recognized this miracle: "*When they saw the courage of Peter and John and realized that they were unschooled, ordinary men, they were astonished and they took note that these men had been with Jesus"* (Acts 4:13).

Would someone looking into your life recognize you were a Christ-follower?

We all love a story of redemption. Examples include fairy tales like "Cinderella," "The Prince and the Toad," "Beauty and the Beast," and popular novels like *A Christmas Carol* (Scrooge is transformed) and movies like "The Matrix." The parable of the Prodigal son (Luke 15) is also a story of redemption and transformation. We are hard-wired to crave redemption and positive change; we revel in seeing good transformations.

Let's dig a little deeper into the scriptures concerning Moses, his transformation, and God's presence. **Read Exodus 33.**

Since this passage is rather long, here is the summary of Exodus 33. It takes place shortly after the Israelites rebelled and worshipped the golden calf, which angered God. He was going to fulfill His commitment to His people by giving them the Promised Land, but God said He would not personally accompany them on the rest of the journey because of His anger toward them.

Moses begged God to continue to dwell with the people in spite of their rebellion. Moses basically said, "If You will not go with us, then don't send us. We want only to be with you. Sending us to the Promised Land with an angel is not the same as having Your presence with us." Moses asked God, "Show me Your glory." This pleased God and He agreed to show Moses a glimpse of Himself and also agreed to continue to dwell with His people.

Let's consider a couple of deep questions about this passage:

- If God spoke to Moses face to face, why did Moses say, "Show me your glory"?

- If God is everywhere (omnipresent), why did He have this conversation with Moses saying His presence would not go with the people to the Promised Land?

These are thought-provoking questions as we try to fully comprehend the concept of God's presence. Our understanding of Him and the meaning of His presence will influence how we behave when we understand the idea of being before God's face.

First, this passage and other Scriptures explain that a man cannot actually see God's face with his own human eyes and live (Exodus 33:20, John 1:18). The verses about Moses speaking to God as a friend and being face to face with God were merely expressions. Modern meteorologists still speak of sundown and sunset although we all know that the earth revolves around the sun. We often say things like, "That seat was as hard as a rock," and everyone understands it is an expression.

Studying carefully the descriptions of Moses and his encounters with God (Exodus 40:34-35), it appears that God's actual glory was hidden in a cloud and that is what Moses saw and how he spoke to God. That was why Moses wanted more, actually to see God in all of His glory. Of course, God explains to Moses that he would die if he actually saw God's face (Exodus 33:20). However, God does arrange for Moses to see Him pass by and get a glimpse of His glory after He passes.

Dallas Willard delivered a lecture entitled, "How is God with Us? How Can We Know It?" He gave this message at Westmont College, and it is available on YouTube.[66] Willard explained there are two ways that God can be with us.

The first way is simply the metaphysical way in which God is omnipresent. He is omnipresent with everyone whether he or she is righteous or irreligious and whether he or she is aware of God's presence or not. There is nothing personal or interactive about the metaphysical presence of God. It is just a fact, like the existence of air in our atmosphere. We breathe the air, and we are really not very aware of it from day to day. People have free will in this life and can simply ignore the reality of God if they choose. One day they will have to acknowledge God and every knee will bow to Christ on that dreadful day (or glorious day depending on your perspective).

The second way God can be with us is by what Willard called "the personal manifestation of His presence." This is very different from just His metaphysical omnipresence. This is "an ongoing interactive relationship ... a walk with us ... a divine blessing."[67]

That is what Moses longed for in Exodus 33. This longing for God's personal presence is at the heart of the spiritual discipline of coram Deo.

A.W. Tozer wrote in a similar fashion about Exodus 33 saying:

"The Presence and the manifestation of the Presence are not the same .... God is here when we are wholly unaware of it .... On our part, there must be surrender .... God will manifest Himself to us, and that manifestation will be the difference between a nominal Christian life and a life radiant with the light of His face."[68]

Willard said the personal manifestation of God's presence has three elements: our perception, His provision, and His power.[69] Moses already was aware of God's presence and spoke with Jehovah often. In Exodus 33, Moses was asking for God's provision and power because just the mere perception that God was present was not sufficient for Moses. He knew the Israelites needed God's provision and power, and without that personal manifestation of God, Moses would rather just stay in the wilderness.

This attitude and mindset that Moses expresses in Exodus 33 is a model for us as we learn the practice of coram Deo. Moses was at a place in his spiritual maturity and relationship with God where he would rather stay in the desert, virtually homeless, than go forward without experiencing God's provision and power in a tangible way (manifestation). If God would not walk down the road with Moses and the Israelites with all of God's glory, provision, and power, then Moses would rather suffer in the desert.

There is another teachable moment for us with regard to Moses and his transformation. He was aware of God's presence as far back as the burning bush or even before. Moses experienced God's presence and became knowledgeable about God's plan for His people (Exodus 3). Yet, Moses was reluctant to obey God at first. Just knowing God's presence and even the particulars of His plan is not necessarily enough for transformation. For Moses, it took living it out, witnessing His power with the ten plagues, experiencing God's purpose in the parting of the Red Sea, tasting the manna from heaven, drinking of water given by God at just the right time, etc.

If the knowledge of God's presence is just in our heads and not in our hearts, we will be like Moses before his transformation. We have to live it out, experience it, and see it for a time; and then it gets into our hearts. Then the Holy Spirit transforms us.

Comparing the before picture of Moses in Exodus 3 to the fully-transformed Moses in Exodus 33 is like looking at a caterpillar before it is transformed into a butterfly. The two images may share the same DNA, but the butterfly is a new creature. Moses wanted God to leave him alone and send someone else in Exodus 3. In contrast, the Moses we see in Exodus 33 was not willing to leave his camp in the desert without God's manifest presence.

The same is true of the transformation of Saul to Paul. Saul was knowledgeable about Jehovah, but his head and heart were totally against Jesus. Saul was determined to bring violence against the church. After his encounter with Jesus on the road to Damascus, Saul began to understand and to experience God in a new way. That is what transformed Saul into the Apostle Paul, a loving servant of Christ, who endured and suffered much for the cause.

This transformation is informative for us. It is a picture of where we need to be in our practice of coram Deo. Our perspective must change as we realize and respond to His presence (chapter 3). We need to heal from our past desert experiences (chapter 4). In addition, we must get our heads cleared in the renewing of our minds and then be filled with the knowledge of God (chapter 5).

In this chapter, we see that we need time to cultivate our heart for God's personal presence. We need to crave God's personal presence in such a way that we are praying daily for His power and purpose in our lives. With our whole being transformed (head and heart), we will be different. It will not happen overnight, but it will happen if we live in His presence.

Just as God used Moses and Paul, God will be able to use us because we will be His obedient servants. Although we have already touched on applying the concepts of transformation, our discussion has now led us to go even deeper into personal application. First, however, let's take a few moments to focus on a couple of brief devotional passages to prepare our hearts for the next section.

Devotional Scripture

Consider the following two passages:

⁴Hear, O Israel: The Lord our God, the Lord is one. ⁵Love the Lord your God with all your heart and with all your soul and with all your strength. ⁶These commandments that I give you today are to be on your hearts. ⁷Impress them on your children. Talk about them when you sit at home and when you walk along the road, when you lie down and when you get up. ⁸Tie them as symbols on your hands and bind them on your foreheads (Deuteronomy 6:4-8).

³⁶"Teacher, which is the greatest commandment in the Law?"

³⁷Jesus replied: "'Love the Lord your God with all your heart and with all your soul and with all your mind.' ³⁸This is the first and greatest commandment. ³⁹And the second is like it: 'Love your neighbor as yourself'" (Matthew 22:36-39).

These passages speak to having a heart for God. As we have studied in the first few chapters, we start with knowing and believing in God as we get our heads around who He is and realizing His presence. The passages above go deeper than knowledge. They tell of a heart and a passion for God like those we saw in the transformed lives of Moses and Paul. After their transformation, they were dedicated to God in every fiber of who they were. That is an amazing, inspiring thought. Visualize yourself transformed like Moses and Paul.

Application/Implication

Maybe you are thinking, "Ok, I want to be transformed. I want to live coram Deo like Moses and Paul. How do I do that? Do I just try really hard? Is there a twelve-step program for me? Is there a *Transformation for Dummies* book? Or is it one of those situations where I am supposed to just let go and let God? How can I be transformed?"

As previous stated about renewing our minds, it is important to understand that we cannot, **by our own power**, change ourselves to the point we are pleasing to God. As we have seen in the cases mentioned earlier, a crucial part of their transformation was an encounter with God; an event in which the person realized he or she was in God's presence (coram Deo). Only God's Holy Spirit can truly **transform** us. God changes us from the inside out, and it is usually not a sudden occurrence.

John Ortberg in his book *The Life You've Always Wanted* compares this gradual transformation to training to run a marathon. He says it is not about "trying real hard" but about steady training in spiritual disciplines under God's coaching. Real transformation does not just happen because we try hard. "There is an immense difference between training to do something and trying to do something .... Spiritual transformation is not a matter of trying harder but of training wisely."[70] (ref: I Timothy 4:7).

In addition, it is important to know there is not one single method that works the same for everyone because each person is different. Ortberg says God made us and it was His design to make us:

> "... wildly, wonderfully, absurdly different from each other. Thinkers and feelers, backslappers and wannabee hermits, racehorses and turtles ... [and] our individual uniqueness means we will experience God's presence and learn to relate to Him in different ways that correspond to our wiring patterns that He Himself created in us."[71]

Ortberg describes these different ways we relate to God as "spiritual pathways." A spiritual pathway "has to do with the way we most naturally sense God's presence and experience spiritual growth."[72]

Consider the following table that describes seven spiritual pathways. We all have some ability to experience God through every one, but usually one or two will come most easily to you.

Spiritual Pathway	Description: "People who naturally walk in this spiritual pathway will ...."	Biblical Example
Intellectual	Draw closer to God as they learn more about Him	The Apostle Paul
Relational	Have a deep sense of God's presence when they're involved in significant relationships with other people	The Apostle Peter
Serving	Discover that God's presence seems more tangible when they are involved in helping others	Martha (friend of Jesus) and Dorcas
Worship	Resonate most naturally to praise and adoration as a means of sensing God's presence	King David
Activist	Have a high level of energy and zeal about spiritual matters and a passion to act	Nehemiah
Contemplative	Love to experience God's presence while they have large blocks of uninterrupted time alone with God	The Apostle John
Creation	Connect with God when they are experiencing the world God made	Jesus

Consider these seven spiritual pathways[73] and make a note of two or three that resonate with you. Use this knowledge to jump-start your spiritual transformation. For example, if you want

100

spiritual transformation and one of the pathways that you relate to is the Creation pathway, then the lesson for you is to take more time experiencing God's creation. This will provide you with more natural opportunities to sense God's presence, draw closer to Him, and experience spiritual transformation. God will honor this kind of intentional action on your part as you prepare your heart and mind for transformation.

Spiritual change is not simple or quick. It is more transformational than completing a college curriculum or achieving a self-help goal like weight loss. Spiritual transformation is life change that will morph us into a new creation. It requires our **complete** commitment.

> [19]My dear brothers and sisters, take note of this: Everyone should be quick to listen, slow to speak and slow to become angry, [20]because human anger does not produce the righteousness that God desires. [21]Therefore, get rid of all moral filth and the evil that is so prevalent and humbly accept the word planted in you, which can save you.

> [22]Do not merely listen to the word, and so deceive yourselves. Do what it says. [23]Anyone who listens to the word but does not do what it says is like someone who looks at his face in a mirror [24]and, after looking at himself, goes away and immediately forgets what he looks like. [25]But whoever looks intently into the perfect law that gives freedom, and continues in it — not forgetting what they have heard, but doing it — they will be blessed in what they do.

> [26]Those who consider themselves religious and yet do not keep a tight rein on their tongues deceive themselves, and their religion is worthless. [27]Religion that God our Father accepts as pure and faultless is this: to look after orphans and widows in their distress and to keep oneself from being polluted by the world (James 1:19-27).

This biblical advice provides practical steps we can take in order to prepare our hearts for transformation. No matter which spiritual pathways resonate with you, an important part of this process begins with looking intently into the Word of God as we discussed in chapter 5.

This is not to say that spiritual transformation is as easy as just reading scripture. Sometimes the transformation comes about by way of an **event** that shakes you to your core as Moses' burning-bush experience or Saul's encounter with Christ on the road to Damascus. It might be a painful desert experience or a God-forsaken low point in your life or a sudden trigger, such as losing a loved one, which can sometimes be a catalyst for change.

Another biblical example is Joseph's story that we have already mentioned. Joseph was a favored son before his brothers sold him into slavery. In the midst of experiencing slavery and prison, Joseph still recognized God's hand of providence. He rose to a position of leadership in Egypt and found within himself the ability to forgive his brothers for their treachery.

This is not to say the event that leads to our transformation must be catastrophic or painful. Sometimes it is a common event. God can use many ways to touch us. Brother Lawrence, in his simple conversations and letters of correspondence to friends, neighbors, and fellow servants, touches on his own transformation. He said that he was an "awkward fellow who broke everything" and that he had a terrible feeling that "God had disappointed him." He said that "he had been long troubled in mind from a certain belief that he should be damned; that [no one] could persuade him to the contrary."[74]

Then one day, when Lawrence was around eighteen years old, a single event changed his life. "That in the winter, seeing a tree stripped of its leaves and considering that within a little time, the leaves would be renewed and after that flowers and fruit would appear."[75]

Brother Lawrence received a realization of the providence and power of God that changed his mind about God. From that time on, he began, little by little, to live in the presence of God, practicing the presence of God. The change didn't happen overnight; but over time, God transformed him.

Life-Change Challenge

The journey of a thousand miles starts with the first step. Let's build on our previous challenges: daily prayer to God, seeking God, thinking of every life experience as a coram Deo moment, approaching Him with reverence and awe as a holy habit, and spending more time in God's Word.

For this challenge, consider your top two spiritual pathways. Meditate on the following key verses that pull several concepts of the last two chapters together:

> [1]*Therefore, I urge you, brothers and sisters, in view of God's mercy, to* **offer your bodies** *as a living sacrifice, holy and pleasing to God — this is your true and proper* **worship**. [2]*Do not conform to the pattern of this world, but* **be transformed** *by the renewing of your mind. Then you will be able to test and approve what God's will is — his good, pleasing and perfect will* (Romans 12:1-2, emphasis mine).

Offering your body as a living sacrifice implies that you must put forward your entire **self** to worship and honor God (head, heart, and soul). The word **worship** implies coming into His presence. Each person can do this in his or her own unique way (spiritual pathways), but there is only so much worshipping you can do **alone**.

Christ's plan was for the church to be a community of believers. Lastly, this verse is about **being** transformed for the purpose of pleasing God. Although we have our part, it is not a **to-do** list to check off. It is about changing to a different state of being, from being worldly to being godly.

Based on all that we have just discussed in this chapter, what steps can you take to transform? How can you heed the Apostle Paul's "urging"? Being more involved and connected to your local church is one of the best ways to pursue your spiritual pathway of choice. Jesus never meant for us to be a bunch of lone wolves. Pray to the Lord that He will reveal His presence to you. Wait expectantly and be ready to offer your entire self in worship to God.

Looking Forward

In the next chapter, we build on the idea of having our heads and our hearts right with God, which leads logically to our habits. We all have specific purposes for our lives. God calls each of us to a specific mission field. The next chapter's focus will be on becoming intentional about our mission and our habits.

Chapter 7: Our Mission

Introduction

God did not create us to chase after trivial matters; our purpose is not fun and games, pursuing the temporary things of this world. Obviously, there is value in rest and recharging, but that is not our purpose or aim in life. As discussed in chapter one, God created mankind special: in His image and designed to have a close relationship with Him. Ephesians 2:10 says that we were created "*for* doing *good works*." It means our purpose on this earth is to do good works in order to bring glory to the name of our Creator (Matthew 5:16).

God has a mission for each of us. As disciples of Christ, we each have a calling. God has given each of us a unique mission. Just as God tasked Adam and Eve with tending their Garden of Eden, He has put us into a microcosm of His creation to tend and care for His creation. The aim of this chapter is to begin to consider the following two questions:

- What is my mission?

- What is my specific purpose?

Some people figure out the answer to those questions early in life. Have you ever known someone who was on a mission? How were they different from most of us?

Bible Study

The topic of figuring out our own mission is very broad. We know that as Christians, we are disciples of Jesus Christ, which means we need to imitate Him. Jesus said in Matthew 20:28 that He did not come to be served but to serve. If Jesus served others, so should we.

> *6We should have the same mind as Christ; Who, being in very nature God, did not consider equality with God something to be used to his own advantage; 7rather, he made himself nothing by taking the very nature of a servant, being made in human likeness. 8And being found in appearance as a man, he humbled himself by becoming obedient to death — even death on a cross!*
>
> *9Therefore God exalted him to the highest place and gave him the name that is above every name, 10that at the name of Jesus every knee should bow, in heaven and on earth and under the earth, 11and every tongue acknowledge that Jesus Christ is Lord, to the glory of God the Father* (Philippians 2:6-11).

Jesus taught His disciples in analogies and word pictures, saying things like you will be "fishers of men" (Matthew 4:19 NASB) and we are to be salt and light in a decaying and dark world (Matthew 5:13-16). He used concrete analogies of the physical world to explain spiritual truths. The Great Commission is the pinnacle of our mission on this earth.

> *18Then Jesus came to them and said, "All authority in heaven and on earth has been given to me. 19Therefore go and make disciples of all nations, baptizing them in the name of the Father and of the Son and of the Holy Spirit, 20and teaching them to obey everything I have commanded*

you. And surely I am with you always, to the very end of the age" (Matthew 28:18-20).

In addition to my fulltime job as an IT Project Manager, I have the privilege to serve as a part-time minister at McDonough Christian Church. Our vision statement indicates how strongly we believe in spiritual growth and discipleship:

> McDonough Christian Church exists to develop devoted followers of Jesus Christ who Love, Imitate, and Duplicate Him in their surrendered lives.

Our vision statement captures the progression of a disciple's spiritual growth with three simple words in order of growth in maturity: **Love, Imitate,** and **Duplicate**. Each one is necessary. One builds on another.

In the **love** phase, a new Christian is falling in love with Jesus, beginning to put away the old self with its bad habits and sinful nature, and beginning to become fully devoted to Christ, making Him Lord in his or her life, one step at a time. The sinful nature is always there, but through God's help, Christians learn no longer to be slaves to it (Romans 7). We also learn that we need to connect to the Lord's church. Chuck Colson warns our spiritual growth must not stop at the personal-obedience stage. He used the phrase "Jesus and Me" to characterize this immature state when a new Christian may not yet be committed to the church.[76]

In the **imitate** stage of spiritual growth, a disciple learns a walk of faith is more than just a personal relationship with Jesus. Being a disciple goes beyond just Jesus and me. We learn to have a Kingdom perspective with a focus on being a productive part of the Body of Christ, the church. We put others' needs above our own and serve unselfishly.

In the **duplicate** phase of spiritual growth, a disciple realizes that a walk of faith involves discipleship. A disciple is someone who learns from and imitates his or her Master. This builds on the Love and Imitate stages and adds **making other disciples**, teaching them to live like Jesus. It is more than just serving others. It is pouring ourselves into others, doing life together in small groups, helping others develop their faith, holding them accountable in love, assisting as they grow in their walk, and ultimately becoming disciple-makers like Jesus.

For the purposes of this chapter's content, we will focus on the place in our Christian journey that lies at the point of transition from **imitate** to **duplicate**. This is a challenging hurdle in the spiritual growth process. It is the step beyond just volunteering. It is the process of learning discipleship in the context of our conscious awareness of God's presence.

In reading the Great Commission, we often focus on the role that we play, and rightly so because this is the area that needs improvement (on our part). However, read Matthew 28:18-20 (printed a few paragraphs back) in the context of coram Deo and God's presence within our mission.

Notice the central fact that Jesus' presence lies at the heart of the process. Matthew 28:18 says God the Father has given all authority to His Son, Jesus. The passage describes the method of making disciples, which includes baptizing in God's name (Father, Son, and Holy Spirit). The disciple is told to make other disciples by teaching new disciples to obey everything Jesus commanded. And perhaps most importantly is the final assurance: *"I will be with you always, to the very end of the age"* which speaks directly to His Presence in this "co-mission": **coram Deo**.

How did Jesus make disciples? Discipleship is like an apprenticeship. It is in some ways like training someone to be just like you; duplicating yourself. And that is one way of describing how Jesus trained His disciples. He poured His life into them, teaching them, modeling the behavior He wanted them to exhibit. He spent months, even years with them. Shouldn't we follow that same example? Shouldn't we share our lives with others as part of our discipleship? That is the critical next step between "imitate" and "duplicate"

Remember our previous discussion about the seven spiritual pathways? (chapter 6)

Although those were manmade and created just to help us discover ways to connect with God and experience His presence, the concept of our uniqueness is both factual and biblical.

Science teaches us that each individual is unique as seen in our faces, our voices, our fingerprints, and our DNA. The Bible teaches us that we are all different parts of one body.

3For by the grace given me I say to every one of you: Do not think of yourself more highly than you ought, but rather think of yourself with sober judgment, in accordance with the faith God has distributed to each of you. 4For just as each of us has one body with many members, and these members do not all have the same function, 5so in Christ we, though many, form one body, and each member belongs to all the others.

6We have different gifts, according to the grace given to each of us. If your gift is prophesying, then prophesy in accordance with your faith; 7if it is serving, then serve; if it is teaching, then teach; 8if it is to encourage, then give encouragement; if it is giving, then give generously; if it is to lead, do it diligently; if it is to show mercy, do it cheerfully.

9Love must be sincere. Hate what is evil; cling to what is good. 10Be devoted to one another in love. Honor one another above yourselves. ¹¹Never be lacking in zeal, but keep your spiritual fervor, serving the Lord. ¹²Be joyful in hope, patient in affliction, faithful in prayer. ¹³Share with the Lord's people who are in need. Practice hospitality (Romans 12:3-13).

This passage speaks of variation as well as unity in the Body.

In John 10:1-5, Jesus uses a beautiful picture of the Good Shepherd and His flock who know His voice. He calls "His own sheep by name and leads them." The Psalmist in Psalm 8 was amazed that our Creator, who created all of heaven and earth, would "be mindful" and "care" for man. In Matthew 10:30 Jesus reveals that not only does God know us but He even knows the trivial things about His children, like the number of hairs on their heads. This does not sound like the distant God that many in our society imply our Creator is. These are deep thoughts about a loving, caring God who is in the details of His children's lives.

Wouldn't a God who loves His children also care deeply about their mission in this life? That is a rhetorical question, and the answer is a resounding **YES**. God cares deeply about His children and our mission in His kingdom. Unfortunately, many of us do not seem to spend very much time focusing on our spiritual mission in life.

John Ortberg uses an analogy as he explains our limited understanding of God and His mission for us. Ortberg says that our lives are like living in a backyard with a high wall or hedge around it; it is so high and dense that we cannot see what's on the outside. The yard represents our known world, and the outside represents eternity. Some people spend their lives completely ignorant or indifferent about what is on the other side of the hedge. Others spend their entire lives obsessed with dreaming about what is on the other side of the walls, to the point that they miss the purpose and meaning of life in the backyard. These are the two extremes.[77]

Continuing with the analogy, consider the high hedges around the backyard and our lack of understanding of what is beyond. Ortberg said:

"Until one day ... a man who looked like all other men made a breathtaking claim. He said he came from the other side of the hedge. He said no one had to be alone anymore. No one has to live in fear. He said a new kind of life — **life with God** — is now available to anyone who wants it. And he didn't bring this life just to give us comfort. He brought it to give us a **mission**. He said anyone who enters this life will join him in becoming carriers of it to others in the backyard. "[78]

That's a powerful analogy from Ortberg. God is with us in our own backyard. Jesus invites us to join Him in a specific mission. Ortberg goes on to say:

"[T]he promise fulfilled in Jesus' coming is the unifying theme of Scripture: Immanuel, 'God with us.' Jesus said, 'Anyone who loves me will obey my teaching. My Father will love them, and we will come to them and make our home with them'."[79]

"God doesn't reveal Himself to us just to make us happy .... [Our mission is to] be conduits of His presence to other people."[80]

That is **coram Deo**!

In summary, with the Great Commission Jesus was giving us a mission to imitate and duplicate Him in order to make disciples. Part of that task is to bring the reality of God's presence and power to others on our side of the hedge using our unique giftedness.

Devotional Scripture

For this chapter's devotional scripture, we will focus on a passage that explains we are called to a life that has eternal importance.

> *3His divine power has given us everything we need for a godly life through our knowledge of him who called us by his own glory and goodness. 4Through these he has given us his very great and precious promises, so that through them you may participate in the divine nature, having escaped the corruption in the world caused by evil desires*
> (II Peter 1:3-4).

First, notice that God gives us this godly life. Second, note the use of the word "participate." This is key. Vine's Greek Dictionary explains that this word **participate** comes from the Greek word *koinonos* an adjective, signifying "having in common."[81] It means that God has chosen to make us His **partners** who will actively participate in a common mission that is divine and eternal. What an incredible privilege and high calling!

> "We were introduced into this 'divine nature' at the time of conversion. Then as we live in the practical enjoyment of God's precious and magnificent promises, we are made more and more conformed to His image." This conformation occurs progressively "the more we behold Him, the more we will become like Him (2Corinthians 3:18) .... the Holy Spirit changes us into His likeness from one degree of glory to another."[82]

Application/Implication

You may say, "So what? What does this mean for me?"

It means that God created you in a unique way. You are one of a kind. And when God created you, He also had a mission in mind for you. He is calling you to that mission.

Jeff Strite posted a sermon on a website called *SermonCentral.com* entitled "Tending Your Garden."[83] Below is an abbreviated adaptation of that sermon which fits well into our current discussion.

Notice that Genesis 2:15 says God called Adam and Eve to the Garden of Eden "to work it and take care of it." It was part of their mission. He did not send them into paradise to bask in the sunshine as if they were on some eternal Hawaiian vacation.

Ephesians 2:10 said that we are created in Christ Jesus to do good works. Ecclesiastes 3 explains that it is a gift of God for us to find satisfaction in our work.

Just as God prepared the Garden of Eden specifically for Adam and Eve, for the purpose of caring for, tending to, and gaining satisfaction from their work, God has given each of us a similar purpose. God has prepared a place in this world for each of us. Our loving Father has designed and prepared for each of us a garden (of sorts). A garden that gives our lives meaning. This is a gift from our Father.

God designed your garden specifically for you. It is the little corner of the world where God wants you to perform good works in His name to bring Glory to Him.

God is at work in creating these gardens every day, creating opportunities for us to do good works. As we surrender to serve Him, He is equipping us with everything we need to successfully tend and care for these gardens. He develops each of us and prepares each of our gardens with our own abilities in mind because He knows our personalities, our characters, our particular strengths, and weaknesses. And no one else is better equipped than you to perform those good works in your garden in pursuing your mission for which God designed you. He created your garden just for you.

God gives each of us little gardens of responsibilities and opportunities. He provides us with a structure and set of guidelines, a Farmer's Almanac (so to speak) to teach us to be faithful in our gardening. Obviously, this book is His Word, the Bible.[84]

What will you do with your garden?

Mother Teresa famously said, "Don't ask God to let you do great things. Instead do small things with great love."

Here are a few questions to ponder.

- What small things can I do to serve God?

- How can I show great love for others in the garden? (your backyard on this side of the hedge)

- What weeds do I need to pull in my garden?

- What seeds am I planting?

- What fruit am I bearing?

- What crop am I harvesting?

"Nobody can do everything; but everybody can do something.

If everybody does something, everything will get done" - Author Unknown

Sarah Young expressed this same sentiment writing as if in the voice of Jesus:

"I am leading you along a way that is uniquely right for you. The closer to Me you grow, the more fully you become your true self – the one I designed you to be. Because you are one of a kind ....Rejoice as we journey together in intimate communion."[85]

What we do to work and tend our garden is up to us. But be aware that doing good works to bring glory to His name is our mission. Making disciples, as Jesus commanded in Matthew 28, is perhaps the greatest good work we can do in our mission in this life. This is our calling and we must not take it lightly. We are not casual tourists chasing after fun in this world God has given us. Instead, we are sharecropping in divine gardening with the Lord (II Peter 1:4). We are partners with Him in a mission with eternal consequences for us and our fellow man. God will not be pleased if — instead of sowing the seed — all we do is sit in our seats. Instead, we need to get busy dong our Father's will: spreading seed (the Gospel), pouring our lives into one another (discipleship), and sharing the harvest of God's presence with everyone, coram Deo!

Remember what Brother Lawrence said: "Let us think often that our only business in this life is to please God."[86]

Life-Change Challenge

Your assignment for this challenge is simple; it pulls together elements from previous chapters. Reflect on what you think your mission is in this world. God has given you certain strengths and placed you in a certain place.

Pray to Him and ask Him to clearly reveal His specific mission to you. Pray that you can see the opportunities that He sends to you in your garden and that you can develop holy habits that will serve His kingdom.

One brief prayer I pray sometimes when I'm wondering what God wants me to be doing in my garden is this:

Father in heaven,

Please give me the wisdom and the will,

Grant me the strength and the skill,

That I need to carry out Your will

In my walk this day. In Christ's name. Amen

Pray that you will realize and respond to His Presence and His calling as you learn the habit of imitating and duplicating His Son.

Looking Forward

In the last three chapters, we've discussed transformation of our heads (chapter 5), hearts (chapter 6), and habits (chapter 7).

In the next three chapters, we will revisit those three general attributes again (head, heart, and habits) but in a new way. The next chapter focuses on the idea of spiritual amnesia.

Chapter 8: Spiritual Amnesia

Introduction

What exactly is spiritual amnesia?

All of us probably know the general meaning of the word "amnesia." Here is the dictionary definition:

> **am·ne·sia** [am-nee-zhuh] <noun> loss of a large block of interrelated memories; complete or partial loss of memory often caused by brain injury, shock, etc. *(dictionary.com)*.

Obviously, spiritual amnesia is different. It occurs when we forget about the One True God and His Marvelous works. It is failing to remember the amazing and miraculous things God has done for us and in us. This is not something that happens all at once like amnesia from a brain injury. Spiritual amnesia is a slow, gradual forgetting. Many times, we are not even aware that this is taking place. But if we are not careful, before long we will find ourselves drifting into spiritual mediocrity, laziness, lukewarmness, compromise, and even excusing our sin by justifying our rebellion against God and His design. That is the case with both examples we will study in this chapter.

God understands how forgetful men and women can be. There are many verses advising the Lord's people to "remember" and "not to forget." Here are just a few:

- **Remember** the Sabbath day, to keep it holy (Exodus 20:8).

- Do **not forget** the things your eyes have seen … teach them to your children …. **Remember** the day you stood before the Lord your God … (Deuteronomy 4:9,10).

- **Remember** that the Lord your God led you on the entire journey these 40 years (Deuteronomy 8:1).

- **Remember** that you were a slave in the land of Egypt and the Lord your God redeemed you (Deuteronomy 15:15).

- **Remember** what Moses the Lord's servant commended you (Joshua 1:12).

- **Remember** His covenant forever — the promise He ordained for a thousand generations (1 Chronicles 16:15).

- I will **remember** the Lord's works; yes, I will **remember** Your ancient wonders. I will reflect on all You have done and meditate on Your actions (Psalm 77:11).

- So **remember** your Creator in the days of your youth (Ecclesiastes 12:1).

- And He took bread, gave thanks, broke it, gave it to them, and said, "This is My body, which is given for you. Do this in **remembrance** of Me" (Luke 22:19).

Why the constant reminder to **remember**? God knows it is easy for us, with our weak minds, to forget very important and necessary spiritual concepts. There is just so much going on all around us in our physical world.

I'm guilty of being distracted and forgetful. During the 2012 holiday season, I agreed to bring the Honey Baked ham to our family Christmas Eve dinner at my mother's home. Two days before the event, I remembered to purchase the delicious entrée. I even remembered to use a coupon! But when my family and I walked in the door at my mother's house, I realized I had forgotten the ham and left it in our refrigerator at home! It was forty-five minutes away. Fortunately, there was a Honey Baked Ham store near my mom's house so we could buy another. Why did I forget? It was my fault but I guess there were just too many distractions and not enough active brain cells.

Bible Study

We will study two prominent examples of believers who at one point in their lives were devoted and obedient to the Lord. Then somehow, at a later time, both of these individuals developed **spiritual amnesia**.

First, let's consider King Saul. Here are a few scriptures that outline Saul's life before he suffered from spiritual amnesia:

- God blessed Saul in his body; he stood head and shoulders above his peers (I Samuel 9:1-2).

- God blessed Saul with His spirit, enabling him to prophesy (I Samuel 10:10).

- God blessed Israel under Saul's leadership to defeat their enemies (I Samuel 11:1-15).

- God chose Saul and anointed him king (I Samuel 9:17; 10:1).

With all of these incredible blessings, you would think King Saul would truly know and live the discipline we call coram Deo. Unfortunately, at some point, King Saul made some serious mistakes and seemed to forget Jehovah God. Instead of living in constant consciousness of his own responsibilities as God's chosen king of Israel, he somehow allowed **spiritual amnesia** to creep in. Here are a few key points that illustrate this serious lapse in King Saul's memory:

- Saul did not obey the Lord in two important situations (I Samuel 13:1-15 and I Samuel 15).

- Saul became jealous of David (I Samuel 18).

- Saul tried to murder David several times (I Samuel 16, 18, 19).

- Saul pursued David and his men in the wilderness (I Samuel 22).

- Saul sought the Witch of Endor in order to speak with the prophet Samuel who was dead (I Samuel 28).

Sadly, King Saul not only suffered from spiritual amnesia, but he had undergone a disgraceful **reverse transformation** from good to bad. In his last years, he was a broken, tormented man.

In a similar fashion, look at what the scriptures reveal about King David. Like Saul, David enjoyed incredible blessings from God. Note the key points below of how Jehovah God blessed King David:

- God protected him against wild beasts when he was a young shepherd (I Samuel 17:34-37).

- God chose David to be the future king of Israel (I Samuel 16).

- God protected him from harm at the hands of King Saul (I Samuel 16, 18, 19).

- God blessed David with Jonathan, a good friend and confidante (I Samuel 20).

- God gave David the foresight not to "dethrone" King Saul (I Samuel 24, 26).

- God granted David victory over his enemies (II Samuel 8 and 10).

- God knew that David had a sincere heart for Him (II Samuel 7).

- God called David "a man after His own heart" (I Samuel 13:14; Acts 13:22).

- God ensured that David would be crowned King of all Israel (II Samuel 2, 5).

No doubt, David was a great man of faith, a man after God's own heart. He was the most admired and powerful man in the land. He was also God's anointed king over Israel. Yet with all of these stunning blessings and advantages, it still wasn't enough to keep David from breaking several of God's commandments. Let's look at the story of David and Bathsheba.

The complete story is in II Samuel 11. For brevity, here is a summary. King David was in his royal palace rather than with his army fighting Israel's enemies. King David was walking on his rooftop and saw Bathsheba bathing on another rooftop nearby. He arranged to have an affair with Bathsheba, who was married to Uriah, a soldier in David's army. Bathsheba became pregnant so David arranged for Uriah to be killed in battle. Then David took Bathsheba to be his own wife.

In this tragic story, we see that David broke at least the following commandments:

- Six: Do not murder.

- Seven: Do not commit adultery.

- Nine: Do not lie.

- Ten: Do not covet.

How do we make sense of this? Why did David make such evil and foolish decisions? Obviously, David suffered from a significant bout of **spiritual amnesia**. He certainly was not living coram Deo. Where was that sincere heart we saw in David when he slew Goliath and when he danced before the Lord with all of his might? It is a shame David did not seem to realize God was present with him on that rooftop when he first lusted for Bathsheba.

As the scriptures reveal, God sent His prophet Nathan to hold David accountable.

Read II Samuel 12. David paid a heavy price for his rebellion in the years following this sin with Bathsheba.

What lessons can we learn from the lives of King Saul and King David?

Is it possible to know the Lord and to be genuinely born again and yet drift away into spiritual amnesia? Is it possible to know forgiveness of sins, possess the gift of eternal life through faith in Jesus Christ, and still drift into a state of spiritual forgetfulness and lukewarmness?

Consider the following passages:

> So, if you think you are standing firm, be careful that you don't fall! (I Corinthians 10:12).

> ⁶I am astonished that you are so quickly deserting the one who called you to live in the grace of Christ and are turning to a different gospel — ⁷which is really no gospel at all. Evidently some people are throwing you into confusion and are trying to pervert the gospel of Christ. ⁸But even if we or an angel from heaven should preach a gospel other than the one we preached to you, let them be under God's curse! ⁹As we have already said, so now I say again: If anybody is

preaching to you a gospel other than what you accepted, let them be under God's curse! (Galatians 1:6-9).

Similar strong language and warnings are also found in Galatians 2:11-14 and 5:1-12.

> *[14]To the angel of the church in Laodicea write: These are the words of the Amen, the faithful and true witness, the ruler of God's creation. [15]I know your deeds, that you are neither cold nor hot. I wish you were either one or the other! [16]So, because you are lukewarm — neither hot nor cold — I am about to spit you out of my mouth.*
>
> *[17]You say, "I am rich; I have acquired wealth and do not need a thing." But you do not realize that you are wretched, pitiful, poor, blind, and naked. [18]I counsel you to buy from me gold refined in the fire, so you can become rich; and white clothes to wear, so you can cover your shameful nakedness; and salve to put on your eyes, so you can see.*
>
> *[19]Those whom I love I rebuke and discipline. So be earnest and repent. [20]Here I am! I stand at the door and knock. If anyone hears my voice and opens the door, I will come in and eat with that person, and they with me.*
>
> *[21]To the one who is victorious, I will give the right to sit with me on my throne, just as I was victorious and sat down with my Father on his throne. [22]Whoever has ears, let them hear what the Spirit says to the churches* (Revelation 3:14-22).

These are sobering words: lukewarm, wretched, blind, spit out.

The answer to the rhetorical questions about whether it is possible for a born-again Christian to suffer from spiritual amnesia is a resounding, "Yes!" If that were not the case, why would we have all these warnings in epistles written to the churches of the first century?

Just as I stated in the preface, this is not a debate over personal salvation. That decision is ultimately in God's hands, and it is futile to debate individual cases. Our study and discussion is about the observable walk of a Christian. I've already discussed the sad story of my own dad and the painful results of his spiritual amnesia. King Saul, King David, and my dad are all examples of believers who developed spiritual amnesia.

What is the remedy for **spiritual amnesia**?

I believe one of the most concise answers to the question is found in a quote from A.W. Tozer, an author who was part of my motivation for this study. Tozer wrote:

> "The world is perishing for lack of the knowledge of God and the Church is famishing for want of **His Presence**. The instant cure of most of our religious ills would be to enter **the Presence** in spiritual experience, to become suddenly aware that we are in God and that God is in us" (emphasis mine).[87]

Devotional Scripture

For this chapter's devotional scripture, we will meditate on a passage that encourages us to focus our minds on the knowledge and wisdom of God:

> [1]*My son, if you accept my words and store up my commands within you, [2]turning your ear to wisdom and applying your heart to understanding — [3]indeed, if you call out for insight and cry aloud for understanding, [4]and if you look for it as for silver and search for it as for hidden treasure, [5]then you will understand the fear of the Lord and find the knowledge of God* (Proverbs 2:1-5).

This passage encourages us to have a hunger and a craving for Godly wisdom and a true understanding of the Lord. This is what was absent in King Saul's and King David's lives at the moments of their downfalls. They were too confident in their own understanding and did not seek knowledge of God. In those low points of their lives, they were not in a state of understanding the fear of the Lord and were not living coram Deo.

Application/Implication

How can we avoid drifting into a state of spiritual amnesia and an ineffectual walk?

A strategy that I have been using is a two-part approach of **Personal Accountability** and **Spiritual Memorials.**

First, read Joshua 4:1-24 which is a about **spiritual memorials**. In this passage, the Israelites cross over the Jordan River into the Promised Land on dry ground. It is an incredibly significant day.

The key verses are verses 21-24:

> *21He said to the Israelites, "In the future when your descendants ask their parents, 'What do these stones mean?' 22tell them, 'Israel crossed the Jordan on dry ground.' 23For the Lord your God dried up the Jordan before you until you had crossed over. The Lord your God did to the Jordan what he had done to the Red Sea when he dried it up before us until we had crossed over. 24He did this so that all the peoples of the earth might know that the hand of the Lord is powerful and so that you might always fear the Lord your God"* (Joshua 4:21-24).

Notice the purpose of this simple stone memorial:

1. It was to **remind** the Israelites it was God who brought them to the Promised Land. This was to cultivate in them and their children, an ongoing, growing faith in God.

Every time they looked upon this Memorial, they could remember God's amazing miracles, and it would inspire and feed their faith in God.

2. It would provide opportunities to **teach** the next generation about the One True God and His Miracles. Read Joshua 4:21-23a. Every time they were with their children and they saw this heap of stones, they were to rehearse the story of how God miraculously brought them into the Promised Land by drying up the Jordan River. *"For the Lord your God dried up the Jordan before you until you crossed over."*

3. It was to **reveal** to all the peoples of the earth that the hand of the LORD (Yahweh) is powerful. Read Joshua 4:24a. Every time the pagan nations that lived in Canaan would hear the story or see this stone memorial, they would be in awe of the God of Israel.

How can we have reminders of God so that we don't end up making the mistakes King Saul and King David made? Has God helped you cross any rivers lately? Removed any barriers for you recently? Has He given you a safe haven to refresh yourself? Maybe you need some **spiritual memorials** to help you **remember** God's blessings. What are some practical ways to have a spiritual memorial?

One thing I do (that many others do as well) is put some of my favorite Scriptures on index cards and put them in my line of sight. For example, on the side of my computer monitor at home, I have this verse:

> *"For I know the plans I have for you," declares the Lord, "plans to prosper you and not to harm you, plans to give you hope and a future"* (Jeremiah 29:11).

This passage memorializes how the Lord helped me conquer my negative thoughts about my career. I'm following God's plan, not the fast track to success. I also keep certain keepsakes and mementos that remind me of wonderful blessings God has done in my life (too numerous to mention here). But sometimes when I feel my Black Dog depression trying to raise its ugly head, I open up that shoebox of mementos and revisit some of my spiritual memorials. This lifts my spirits and reminds me of God's provision.

The second strategy for combating spiritual amnesia is through **personal accountability** to the community of faith (the church). Just as in participating in an exercise program or pursuing a new career, it helps to have a partner or a support team. If you are accountable to someone, you are more likely to keep your commitments and be successful. God understood this when He created the church.

Read a few **one another** passages like John 13:34-35; Romans 12:1-16; James 5:13-16. These and other passages regarding the church, indicate that God's great design was for a close-knit community of believers that shared everything, both blessings and burdens. Are you taking advantage of God's design? Or are you trying to figure it out on your own? You need the Body of Christ. Your accountability partner can be a spiritual mentor, an accountability partner, a believing spouse, or just a godly friend.

As I mentioned earlier, one of the ways I serve in the church is to help coordinate community groups. Many churches call them **small groups,** which seems to be the most common name. My role is to facilitate placing new church members or even visitors in a community group that meets in a home near them on a night that is convenient to them. These groups are more than a home Bible study group. They are like extended family for fellowship, accountability, encouragement, and ultimately discipleship. Along with coordinating these groups, I also lead one and attend another. I have a couple of guys in these groups that I can share my struggles with and who help bear my burdens. That keeps me accountable.

King David had Jonathan as his friend and confidante. At a certain low point in David's life, when he had been running and hiding from King Saul for a long time, David's strength was failing. Enter David's best friend, Jonathan. Let's look at the passage:

> [15]While David was at Horesh in the Desert of Ziph, he learned that Saul had come out to take his life. [16]And Saul's son Jonathan went to David at Horesh and helped him find strength in God. [17]"Don't be afraid," he said. "My father Saul will not lay a hand on you. You will be king over Israel, and I will be second to you. Even my father Saul knows this." [18]The two of them made a covenant before the Lord. Then Jonathan went home, but David remained at Horesh (I Samuel 23:15-18).

Do you have a Jonathan in your life who can help you find strength and point you back to God? My Jonathan is my good friend named Nick. We talk and share our victories and burdens at least weekly. We are accountable to each other. That is how God intended us to live.

Are you a member of a community group (or small group) that encourages you, fellowships with you, and holds you accountable in love? That is God's design. It is not for us to be a spectator in a huge cathedral with a fifty-piece orchestra and the most eloquent preacher. God's design for the church was more about accountability and discipleship.

Disclaimer: Please don't get me wrong. Corporate worship is very important. Acts 2:42-47 and Acts 5:12 reveal that the church met together in a big group (at Solomon's Colonnade). But notice is says they also met in small groups in their homes. Our modern church in America sometimes emphasizes and celebrates the **big group** meeting and neglects the **small group** meetings. We need both in order to follow His design for the Body of Christ.

David also had the prophet Nathan who held him accountable and was not afraid to speak the truth into his life. We see this at the end of the affair with Bathsheba. We have already discussed a modern equivalent of this in chapter 3 of this study of coram Deo: Rich Mullins had his friend and accountability partner, Beaker, who travelled with him, wrote songs with him, shared his life with him, and helped keep Rich out of trouble in Amsterdam.

Who is holding you accountable? Do you have a Nathan, Jonathan, or Beaker in your life?

This two-pronged strategy of **spiritual memorials** and **personal accountability** can help us remember who we are and whose we are.

> "The best way to keep the enemy out is to keep Christ in. The sheep need not be terrified by the wolf; they have but to stay close to the shepherd. It is not the praying sheep Satan fears but **the presence of the shepherd.**"[88]

The goal of this study is to share practical strategies to learn the spiritual discipline of coram Deo. As previously stated, coram Deo is about living in the presence of God, always realizing that we are before God's face in every moment of every day.

Max Lucado says, "Wherever you are. Whatever time it is .... you are only a decision away from the **presence of your Father.**"[89] In the Lord's Prayer, Christ has provided "more than a model for prayer, he has provided a **model for living**. These words do more than just tell us **what to say** to God; they tell us **how to exist with God**" (emphasis mine).[90]

Life-Change Challenge

This life-change challenge is straightforward: We need to adopt a strategy to combat **spiritual amnesia**. Just as God instructed the Israelites when they crossed the Jordan, each of us should create our own **spiritual memorials** to stay mindful of what God has done for us. It might be as detailed as keeping a journal or as easy as writing a verse of scripture on an index card and taping it to your mirror or your car console to remind you of something meaningful. It will be a memorial to God's faithfulness. This will help bring God's presence to mind — **coram Deo.**

Secondly, if you don't already have one, please find someone in your life who can be your **accountability partner** or confidante. God's design is for us to share our lives in a close relationship with Him and a close relationship with His church. Doing life together is the way the early church functioned. If you do not have an accountability partner, pray for the Lord to send someone into your life to serve as your confidante. We need to get back to God's great design.

Looking Forward

In chapter nine, we will discuss the blessing of serving an awesome, loving God. The primary scripture to study is Psalm 139, a passage that will touch your heart and cause you to draw near to your Father in the discipline of coram Deo.

Chapter 9: Serving an Awesome God

Introduction

Earlier we saw how church reformers such as Martin Luther understood and truly lived the discipline of coram Deo, living in God's presence. The early church understood and lived it as well as saw firsthand the life-changing, history-altering effects of the outpouring of the Holy Spirit.

Perhaps the earliest extant Christian writing is a book called *First Clement.* (*Extant* simply means outside the accepted cannon of inspired Scripture). Some Christians believe *First Clement* is inspired. Either way, this valuable manuscript gives us a window into the faith and thinking of the early church.

Clement of Rome wrote:

> "Since, therefore, all things are seen and heard, let us fear Him and abandon the abominable lusts that spawn evil works, in order that we may be shielded by His mercy from the coming judgments. For where can any of us escape from His mighty hand?" (I Clement 28:1).[91]

Then, Clement quotes from perhaps one of the most amazing Bible passages: Psalm 139.

Read Psalm 139.

This psalm is my wife's favorite Bible passage. Terri's mother conceived her out of wedlock. My wife never knew her father. As a young adult, a relative told Terri that when her mother found out she was pregnant, someone offered to help her get an abortion. This person had helped his own daughter get an abortion earlier for an inconvenient pregnancy. Fortunately, Terri's mother chose to keep the baby. So this passage reminds my wife of how God watched over her while she was in her mother's womb. I shudder to think of what a huge loss it would have been if Terri had been aborted. My wife has been such a joy and a blessing to so many people.

Clement goes on to give the first-century church some advice that we should listen to as well: "Let us therefore approach Him in holiness of soul, lifting up to Him pure and undefiled hands, loving our gentle and compassionate Father who made us His chosen portion" (I Clement 29:1).[92] Clement's words sound like some of the key points discussed in chapter 1 and chapter 4: God wants a close relationship with us because, even though it doesn't make sense to us, we humans are precious to God. This is truly an astonishing realization.

Bible Study

Studying Psalm 139 is instrumental in fully grasping the principles of coram Deo. This psalm is a beautiful prayer to God, asking Him to examine the writer's heart and see its true devotion. The writer claims his loyalty to his Creator in a style reminiscent of Job. The language is poetic and emotional. The psalmist expresses a profound awareness of how awe inspiring God is as the writer asks God literally to look into his soul. The verses profess that God already knows every thought, every word, and every deed. The psalmist also proclaims that there is no hiding from God who has literally been witness to the writer's formation, concealed in his mother's womb.

The psalm consists of four poetic paragraphs, each with six verses (1-6, 7-12, 13-18, and 19-24). Each paragraph elaborates on the central theme: we serve an awesome God.

Tradition and most scholars agree that this psalm is "Of David" meaning it was written by King David around 1000 B.C.

Reread verses 1-6 (the first paragraph of this psalm):

1You have searched me, Lord, and you know me.

2You know when I sit and when I rise; you perceive my thoughts from afar.

3You discern my going out and my lying down; you are familiar with all my ways.

4Before a word is on my tongue you, Lord, know it completely.

5You hem me in behind and before, and you lay your hand upon me.

6Such knowledge is too wonderful for me, too lofty for me to attain (Psalm 139:1-6).

Notice David writes this as a personal address or prayer to God. These verses proclaim that God knows the heart of the King. There was a cultural concept of the ancient world that no one could look into the heart of a king. Proverbs 25:3 says that the hearts of kings are unsearchable. So to say that David's god knew his heart was a very bold statement. By implication, if God can know even the heart of King David, He certainly knows our hearts. This means that God is omniscient or all-knowing. This is such a deep and almost overwhelming thought that it amazes the psalmist. The thoughts are just "too wonderful for me" because it is just beyond human understanding.

Reread verses 7-12 (Paragraph 2):

>*7Where can I go from your Spirit? Where can I flee from your presence?*

>*8If I go up to the heavens, you are there; if I make my bed in the depths, you are there.*

>*9If I rise on the wings of the dawn, if I settle on the far side of the sea,*

>*10even there your hand will guide me, your right hand will hold me fast.*

>*11If I say, "Surely the darkness will hide me and the light become night around me,"*

>*12even the darkness will not be dark to you; the night will shine like the day, for darkness is as light to you* (Psalm 139:7-12).

Now, David proclaims that there is no hiding from God, no escaping from His divine Presence. The modern term is omnipresence. To illustrate the concept of omnipresence, David describes God's presence in spatial terms: above and below (heaven and the depth) and east to west (wings of dawn in the east and far side of the sea as west).

This omnipresence is not something that David dreads but is seen in the context of a loving God who will "guide me ... hold me fast" through His inescapable supervision. Even the darkness does not conceal us from God.

Reread verses 13-18 (Paragraph 3):

>*13For you created my inmost being; you knit me together in my mother's womb.*

14I praise you because I am fearfully and wonderfully made; your works are wonderful, I know that full well.

15My frame was not hidden from you when I was made in the secret place, when I was woven together in the depths of the earth.

16Your eyes saw my unformed body; all the days ordained for me were written in your book before one of them came to be.

17How precious to me are your thoughts, God! How vast is the sum of them!

18Were I to count them, they would outnumber the grains of sand — when I awake, I am still with you (Psalm 139:13-18).

Here David gives God full credit for his life and, by implication, all life. Not only did God create life for the psalmist, but David also sees God as intimately involved in every detail, literally putting him together in the womb and ordaining the length of his life before birth. He sees God as the divine life-giver, creation architect, and circumstance engineer. Knowledge of God's awesome power is sobering and even a bit frightening: "... fearfully and wonderfully ... wonderful." This section describes God as all-powerful or omnipotent. Such attributes inspire a rational believer to view God with awe and wonder and to react by praising Him.

Reread verses 19-24 (Paragraph 4):

19If only you, God, would slay the wicked! Away from me, you who are bloodthirsty!

20They speak of you with evil intent; your adversaries misuse your name.

21Do I not hate those who hate you, Lord, and abhor those who are in rebellion against you?

²²I have nothing but hatred for them; I count them my enemies.

²³Search me, God, and know my heart; test me and know my anxious thoughts.

²⁴See if there is any offensive way in me, and lead me in the way everlasting (Psalm 139:19-24).

In these verses, David is swearing his allegiance to God, the Father. He professes his zeal for God and sets himself up against God's enemies such as those who misuse His name.

Some commentators have noted that verses 21-22 contain a declaration of loyalty that echoes the pledge required by ancient kings of their vassals. In ancient times, kings would require that their vassals must agree with the royal proclamation: "With my friend you shall be a friend, and with my enemy you shall be an enemy."

The psalm ends in a tone that echoes how it began: "Examine me, see the integrity of my devotion, and keep me true."

When I think about the incredible devotion that David must have felt in his spirit as he wrote those words, I am amazed. I aspire to have that same transparency and devotion. How desperately the body of Christ needs to have that same heart and dedication to our Father.

In what ways do we (mankind in general) still try to find ways to hide from God or to somehow doubt (through words or actions) that God is who He says He is?

What are some ways that we can live a life like David proclaims in this psalm?

Devotional Scripture

Before we go too far down the road of personal application, let's spend a few minutes reading and reflecting on another Psalm of David in the context of Psalm 139 and coram Deo. The Lord the Shepherd of His People: A Psalm of David.

¹The Lord is my shepherd; I shall not want.

²He makes me to lie down in green pastures; He leads me beside the still waters.

³He restores my soul; He leads me in the paths of righteousness For His name's sake.

⁴Yea, though I walk through the valley of the shadow of death, I will fear no evil; For You are with me; Your rod and Your staff, they comfort me.

⁵You prepare a table before me in the presence of my enemies; you anoint my head with oil; My cup runs over.

⁶Surely goodness and mercy shall follow me all the days of my life; And I will dwell in the house of the Lord Forever (Psalm 23, NKJV).

Reading this, another beautiful piece of poetry, in the context of Psalm 139 gives us a true feeling of God's love that ties all the way back to His original design. He created us to have a close personal relationship with Him. The pasture in Psalm 23 is reminiscent of the Garden of Eden. The psalmist finds reassurance in the fact his Good Shepherd is with him even in the difficult valleys of life as we discussed in chapter 4.

And the most encouraging and inspiring message to glean from this passage is that, as disciples of Christ, we share in these blessings today, right now, as well as the promise at the end of the psalm concerning dwelling with the Lord forever. We don't have to wait to dwell in His presence. The benefit of living coram Deo is that we are living with Him right now! Praise the Lord!

Application/Implications

Thinking back on Psalm 139 and how it speaks of God as our loving creator who is all-powerful, all-knowing, and always present, let's spend a few moments of personal reflection.

What practical steps can we take today to be a more devoted servant of God? Do your actions reflect someone who understands and truly believes that God is omniscient, omnipresent, and omnipotent? Would you describe your devotion to God as emphatically as this psalmist has done? If not, why not?

One additional scripture that I believe complements the passages we have just studied in Psalms comes from the book of Numbers. The context is the Israelites are on the road to the Promised Land. The specific timing is the dedication of the tabernacle. God is giving very detailed instructions to Moses to train the priests (Aaron and his sons) on how properly to bless God's people. The passage is referred to as the Priestly Blessing or Aaronic Blessing:

> [22]The Lord spoke to Moses: [23]Tell Aaron and his sons: You will bless the Israelites as follows. Say to them:
>
> [24]The Lord bless you and protect you.
>
> [25]The Lord make his face shine on you and be gracious to you.
>
> [26]The Lord lift up his face to you and grant you peace.

27They will place my name on the Israelites, and I will bless them (Numbers 6:22-27 CEB).

Why would God care enough to give specific instructions to the priests? Why would the Creator of the universe care to specify the exact wording that the priests should say in order to bless the Israelites?

I don't mean to sound like a broken record, but I believe the answer goes all the way back to His design. God wants a personal relationship with His people. The Law of Moses was one of the steps to lead His people back into a personal relationship with Him. The Law of Moses, with its rituals that included things like high priests, sacrificial lambs, Passover, feasts, etc., would set up a foreshadowing that would teach the people about Messiah. Through the Chosen One, the Messiah, God would redeem His people once and for all.

But in the passages we have read, we hear loud and clear the love of a heavenly Father who is in pursuit of a prodigal son (humanity). It is almost like a love song written about us, penned by our spiritual forefathers to tell us how much God loves us. These passages are written from different perspectives but the core message is the same in the praise and adoration of God because He loves us against all logic:

> *You know me [everywhere]. Your hand will guide me....Your eyes saw my unformed body* (Psalm 139).

> *He leads me .... My cup runs over ...* (Psalm 23).

> *The Lord bless you and protect you. The Lord make his face shine on you and be gracious to you. The Lord lift up his face to you and grant you peace* (Numbers 6).

And then at the end of the Aaronic Blessing, God promises to bless us, all those who wear His name: *"They will place my name on the Israelites, and I will bless them. "*

These three passages are incredible. When we come to see God's unfathomable love for fallen humanity, it boggles the mind. Does this encourage you? Does it inspire you? I know it is such a blessing to me. Praise the Lord for His love for us. I know I don't deserve it. What about you?

After you take in and process these scriptures that testify to God's unfailing and boundless love for us, how do you feel? Does any of it touch your soul and inspire you to live differently?

Would other people observe your life and see a devoted believer as awestruck by his or her Lord as the Psalmist who wrote Psalm 23 and 139 was? It makes me want to share this with someone else. I just simply can't help but praise Him when I come to realize His love for me.

Life-Change Challenge

Our God is such a loving caring God who sees us and has always seen us. He is omniscient, omnipresent, and omnipotent. For this challenge, there are two very simple parts:

1. Add a new element to your prayers. As you continue to pray and develop the holy habit of coram Deo, pray for the Lord to examine you just as David prayed in Psalm 139. Acknowledge and praise God for who He is and pray for a **pure heart**. Pray the Holy Spirit will reveal and convict you regarding the areas of your life that need to change. Pray for the honesty and transparency David expressed in this psalm. How different our world would be if just a fraction of believers met this challenge. The result would be contagious and spread like wildfire.

2. The second element is simple and fun. Having a thankful heart can be the wind beneath your wings. Being thankful can lift your spirits and pump up your zeal for the Lord. I challenge you to make a simple list of 101 things you are thankful for right now. Start with what you are thankful for today and this week. Think back on God's blessings and answered prayers. Write them down. Make a thankful list and check it more than twice. If you get stuck before you get to 101, think further back in time. Also think of timeless things that you are thankful for, like family members and God's creation.

On my list I have all kinds of things (in no particular order here); from Amy, my daughter, to annual bonuses, Bibles, bananas and Coca-Cola; from Matthew, my son, to my mom to mission trips. I'm thankful for my wife, my job, and my health. I'm grateful for peanut butter, Prilosec (heartburn medicine), and cell phones. I thank God for our wonderful family vacations and thank Him for great Christian writers like Colson, Dobson, Lewis, Lucado, and Ortberg. I am pleased about the 5K and 10K races I barely finished and value my slowly- appreciating 401(k).

My thankful list is eclectic and gloriously long. I'm so thankful for every single person and thing on the list. I recognize that these good gifts are blessings from above (James 1:17). Some of the items cause me to choke back tears. Others bring a chuckle or warm-fuzzy, joyful feelings. It is like a scrapbook of God's incredible blessings personalized for me. As mentioned in chapter 4, Dr. Dobson said, "For reasons that are impossible to explain, we human beings are incredibly precious to God."[93]

My list convinces me that He particularly loves me. Your thankful list will make you feel the same way. Have fun with this life-change challenge and live coram Deo every day.

Looking Forward

The next chapter will further elaborate on making His Presence felt in our lives on a day-to-day basis, making the discipline of coram Deo part of who we are. It will stress the need to walk in His Presence today.

Chapter 10: His Presence in Our Present

Introduction

There is a modern day tale told by numerous ministers over the years about Satan holding a demonic convention. Various versions of this can be found in numerous sources. Here is my own slightly abbreviated adaptation of this tale.

In Satan's opening address at his demon convention, he said, "We can't keep the disciples of Christ from going to church. We can't keep them from reading their Bibles and knowing the truth. We can't even keep Christians from forming an intimate, abiding relationship with Christ. Satan asked, "How are we going to defeat the church?"

One demon suggested more persecution. But Satan explained that the church has historically thrived in response to persecution.

Another demon suggested famine and financial struggles. Satan again rejected the idea and sited historical examples when the church pulled together and grew during lean times.

Then a demon stood up and suggested: "Let's distract the church and keep them busy."

"How do you suggest we do this?" Satan asked.

"Keep them busy in the nonessentials of life and invent innumerable schemes to occupy their minds," the demon answered. "Tempt them to spend and borrow like there is no tomorrow so that they create a lifestyle they can't afford. Persuade them to work long hours, working six or seven days a week, twelve to fifteen hours a day, in an attempt to keep up with their costly lifestyles. Keep them from spending time with their children and spouses.

"As their families fragment, soon their homes will offer no escape from the pressures of work. Over stimulate their minds so they cannot hear that still small voice. Pound their minds with the news twenty-four hours a day. Have ads and information pop up constantly on their computers and phones. Flood their mailboxes with junk mail, phony sweepstakes, and every kind of newsletter and promotional offering free products, cheap services, and false hopes. Even in their recreation, let them be excessive with violent games and neverending sports, season after season, to entice them to never go out in nature to reflect on God's wonders. Convince them that fun can only be found in sporting events, profane movies, obscene art, and every manner of possession from luxury cars to huge TV's to grand homes to fancy phones, things that are costly and ever changing."

Satan said, "That will work! Go at once! Make it happen!"

It was quite a demonic convention in the end. The demons went eagerly to their assignments ... the question is, "Has the devil been successful in his schemes?"[94]

Distraction and busyness are perhaps the most underestimated plight of our generation. John Ortberg wisely said:

> "If you are going to be **with God** at all, you must be with Him now — in this **moment**. That is why the psalmist says, 'This is the day the Lord has made; let us rejoice and be glad in it." (emphasis mine)[95]

In this chapter, we will consider the topic of sensing His presence in our present (our everyday routine). We will discuss the idea of walking with God, moment by moment. We will also explore the reality that mature disciples yearn for God, hungering and thirsting after Him. This is how we fight against Satan's schemes of distraction and busyness that block our ability to live coram Deo.

> *Today, if you hear His voice, do not harden your hearts . . . .*
> *But encourage one another daily, as long as it is called*
> *"today"* (Hebrews 3:7, 8a, 13a, emphasis mine).

Have you ever really appreciated the blessings God was giving you while you were in the moment, not distracted or taking them for granted? Was there a time in your life when you really had a moment of reflection and you thought to yourself, "I'm so glad the Lord allowed me to recognize and cherish this moment while I'm in it?"

Between 1998 and 2001, I experienced a wonderful time of **bliss** in my life (for lack of a better word). My wife and children were healthy and happy. We were content in the church we were attending and able to serve in a meaningful way. I had a fantastic job as a technical training consultant working for a profitable IT company. I had found my career niche where I could be very effective, which gave me upward mobility, and which was rewarding me with a good income. It was before the attacks on 9/11. At that time, occasional air travel could still be somewhat enjoyable. I travelled about twenty-five percent of the time. I was racking up frequent flyer miles and hotel points. This in turn enabled me to redeem those points to take my family on some great vacations that I normally could not afford.

I distinctly remember numerous times during those years when I was reflective and just kept thinking how blessed I was in so many ways: my family, my health, my faith, my career. I remember praying and being so thankful for God's blessings. It was a time when I was learning to live in God's presence before I had ever heard of coram Deo. I am so glad that God allowed me to recognize that time of blessing and cherish those moments.

I've had other reflective moments since that time, but those years were the first of that kind of intense reflection when I was so appreciative for that moment in time. I had a sense that it was a special time, and it was. The key is to live in the moment and be thankful even when it is not a blissful moment. The Apostle Paul calls it the **secret** of contentment (Philippians 4:10-13).

Bible Study

Let's read about a few examples of biblical figures who knew how to trust God and live in the moment with God, and see what we can **glean** from the Lord's Word. To glean means to harvest something a little bit at a time.

Enoch

Enoch was a faithful servant of God who lived a few generations before the Flood.

> *21When Enoch had lived 65 years, he became the father of Methuselah. 22After he became the father of Methuselah, Enoch walked faithfully with God 300 years and had other sons and daughters. 23Altogether, Enoch lived a total of 365 years. 24Enoch walked faithfully with God; then he was no more, because God took him away* (Genesis 5:21-24).

> *5By faith Enoch was taken from this life, so that he did not experience death: "He could not be found, because God had taken him away." For before he was taken, he was commended as one who pleased God. 6And without faith it is*

146

impossible to please God, because anyone who comes to him must believe that he exists and that he rewards those who earnestly seek him (Hebrews 11:5-6).

Based on these passages, we can see that Enoch had great faith and was faithful to God on a long-term basis. It says he walked with God.

Matthew Henry wrote:

"Two cannot walk together except they be agreed, Amos 3:3 ....To walk with God, is to set God always before us, to act as always under his eye. It is constantly to care, in all things to please God, and in nothing to offend him."[96]

That sounds like practicing the presence of God or coram Deo.

What do you think the Holy Spirit is telling us about Enoch?

How can we apply this to our own walk?

This is the message we have heard from him and declare to you: God is light; in him there is no darkness at all. 6If we claim to have fellowship with him and yet walk in the darkness, we lie and do not live out the truth. 7But if we walk in the light, as he is in the light, we have fellowship with one another, and the blood of Jesus, his Son, purifies us from all sin (I John 1:5-7).

We need faith to please God. Enoch's story is short and simple. We do not need to complicate it. Enoch walked in agreement with God, he walked in the light of God's presence and experienced close fellowship with God. We must have faith and learn to walk with God daily as an act of surrender. We must appreciate God's presence in all circumstances.

Other passages about walking with God:

- Psalm 89:15

- Prov.13:20

- Micah 6:8

Elijah

Elijah was a faithful prophet of God in the northern kingdom of Israel during the reign of evil King Ahab around 850 B.C. We best remember him for defending the worship of Yahweh in his showdown with the priests of the Canaanite god Baal on Mount Carmel (I Kings 18).

The specific scripture we will focus on documents what happened after Mount Carmel, after Queen Jezebel threatened Elijah's life. God protected Elijah by sending him into hiding. God was providing for Elijah using the water of a brook and using ravens to bring him food. Then the brook dried up.

> *⁷Some time later the brook dried up because there had been no rain in the land. ⁸Then the word of the Lord came to him: ⁹"Go at once to Zarephath in the region of Sidon and stay there. I have directed a widow there to supply you with food." ¹⁰So he went to Zarephath. When he came to the town gate, a widow was there gathering sticks. He called to her and asked, "Would you bring me a little water in a jar so I may have a drink?" ¹¹As she was going to get it, he called, "And bring me, please, a piece of bread."*

> *¹²"As surely as the Lord your God lives," she replied, "I don't have any bread — only a handful of flour in a jar and a little olive oil in a jug. I am gathering a few sticks to take home and make a meal for myself and my son, that we may eat it — and die."*

¹³Elijah said to her, "Don't be afraid. Go home and do as you have said. But first make a small loaf of bread for me from what you have and bring it to me, and then make something for yourself and your son. ¹⁴For this is what the Lord, the God of Israel, says: 'The jar of flour will not be used up and the jug of oil will not run dry until the day the Lord sends rain on the land.'"

¹⁵She went away and did as Elijah had told her. So there was food every day for Elijah and for the woman and her family. ¹⁶For the jar of flour was not used up and the jug of oil did not run dry, in keeping with the word of the Lord spoken by Elijah.

¹⁷Some time later the son of the woman who owned the house became ill. He grew worse and worse, and finally stopped breathing. ¹⁸She said to Elijah, "What do you have against me, man of God? Did you come to remind me of my sin and kill my son?"

¹⁹"Give me your son," Elijah replied. He took him from her arms, carried him to the upper room where he was staying, and laid him on his bed. ²⁰Then he cried out to the Lord, "Lord my God, have you brought tragedy even on this widow I am staying with, by causing her son to die?" ²¹Then he stretched himself out on the boy three times and cried out to the Lord, "Lord my God, let this boy's life return to him!"

²²The Lord heard Elijah's cry, and the boy's life returned to him, and he lived. ²³Elijah picked up the child and carried him down from the room into the house. He gave him to his mother and said, "Look, your son is alive!"

²⁴Then the woman said to Elijah, "Now I know that you are a man of God and that the word of the Lord from your mouth is the truth" (I Kings 17:7-24).

Notice how Elijah understood that God is involved in our everyday lives; even the so-called trivial parts of life like our daily bread. Another significant fact: This is the first instance of raising the dead recorded in Scripture. Notice the very revealing last statement that the widow made in verse 24:

> *"Now I know that you are a man of God and that the word of the Lord from your mouth is the truth"*

Think about the power of her words and the insight it gives us. What picture does it paint? She recognizes this miracle of God performed by Elijah, and she recognizes that the word of God is truth and it is coming to her through the physical mouth of Elijah. He is, in a sense, the conduit between God and the widow. We might draw it out like this:

What can we glean from this passage? One important thing to glean from Elijah's testimony is that our job is to bring God's Word to the people in our lives. We, like Elijah, are just ordinary people (James 5:16-18). God sends us opportunities to share our faith with people like this widow who did not know God. We encounter lost and disconnected people all the time. Common statements about these encounters with unbelievers go something like this:

- You may be the only "Jesus" some people ever see.

- You may be the only Bible someone ever reads.

These statements are true. We need to learn that He will send us opportunities where we can be the conduit for His message to the world. It might start with something as simple as a smile or being kind or courteous to someone. It could be as significant as sharing our faith with someone over an extended period or having someone recognize God's Word coming out of our mouths. Are we praying for God to use us like this?

The Psalmist

The Psalmist truly had a passion for God. These passages complement the heart of Jesus' sermon on the mount (Matthew 5-7) where He made statements like, "*Blessed are those who hunger and thirst after righteousness for they will be filled.*" Here is what the psalmist said about his walk with God:

¹How lovely is your dwelling place, Lord Almighty!

²My soul yearns, even faints, for the courts of the Lord; my heart and my flesh cry out for the living God.

³Even the sparrow has found a home, and the swallow a nest for herself, where she may have her young — a place near your altar, Lord Almighty, my King and my God.

⁴Blessed are those who dwell in your house; they are ever praising you.

¹⁰Better is one day in your courts than a thousand elsewhere; I would rather be a doorkeeper in the house of my God than dwell in the tents of the wicked (Psalm 84:1-4; v.10).

¹As the deer pants for streams of water, so my soul pants for you, my God.

²My soul thirsts for God, for the living God. When can I go and meet with God?

³My tears have been my food day and night, while people say to me all day long, "Where is your God?"

⁴These things I remember as I pour out my soul: how I used to go to the house of God under the protection of the Mighty One with shouts of joy and praise among the festive throng (Psalm 42:1-4).

What can we glean from these psalms? A faithful child of God yearns for the Father. This psalmist shares the same heart for God that we see in Hebrews 11, a passage that celebrates those people who lived by faith, struggling as aliens in this world, **longing** for a "better country — a heavenly one" (Hebrews 11:16). The psalmist is a person of faith we should strive to emulate.

Just as Jesus Christ constantly prayed to God, we should cry out to our Father. Our lives should display a true thirst for Him. A true disciple of Christ who has this kind of passion and a sincere heart for the Lord will stand out from most of his peers who are more casual in their faith.

For further study, consider the fate of the Apostles. Read the book of Acts. As the apostles lived out their faith and lived what we call coram Deo, their lives caught the attention of everyone around them (Acts 4:13). The acts of the apostles, through the hand of the Holy Spirit, brought glory to Christ and the ultimate result was a changed world.

In II Timothy 4:8, the Apostle Paul reflects back on his life of service, dedication, and sacrifice for the cause of Christ. He says that now he awaits his reward. And Paul states that such a reward awaits everyone who is **truly longing** for the Lord's appearing.

Bestselling author Richard Foster wrote *Streams of Living Water*. It is inspired by the words of Jesus: "Out of the believer's heart shall flow rivers of living water" (John 7:38). Foster's premise is that over the years, "certain precious teachings or vital experiences" that God intended for the church have been neglected.[97]

The Holy Spirit has ordained that believers and groups of people have been raised up "to correct the omission." But due to sectarianism and denominationalism, "the renewed teaching ... [encounters] resistance ... and is denounced ... and [becomes isolated] from other Christian communities."[98]

Foster details six great traditions of the church, which includes one that fits well with this study on coram Deo. Foster calls it the "Incarnation Tradition," paraphrased below, which pulls several things together from previous sections of our study.

The Incarnation Tradition

Foster quotes Susanna Wesley, mother of John and Charles Wesley, who prayed, "Help me, Lord, to remember that religion is not to be confined to the church, or closet, nor exercised only in prayer and meditation, but that **everywhere I am in Thy presence.**"[99]

The sacraments of the church demonstrate God's use of matter to make present and visible the invisible realm of the Spirit. God grafts us into the church by burying and then raising us up in Baptism, and God continually feeds us by enacting the death and resurrection of Christ in the Communion service, or Eucharist.

We are to take our Christian faith and incorporate it into every aspect of our daily lives, into our homes, into our work, into our relationships, and, yes, even into our dealings with our enemies. Colossians 3:17 says, *"Whatever you do, work at it with all your heart, as working for the Lord, not for men."*

In the middle of our workday world is where people desperately need to see the reality of God made visible and manifest. If we allow Him, the Holy Spirit continually moves in us and among us as our ever-present Teacher and Mentor.

God is truly among us. The world is "charged" with the grandeur of God.[100] "God stoops to our needs and allows Himself to be glimpsed in the material world."[101] The very **presence of God** is manifest in the smallest, most mundane of daily activities.

We are weak, **forgetful, distracted,** and confused. The Sacraments "**shock us** back into reality by making specific and concrete our Christian identity."[102]

God calls us to surrender our lives to Him and "allow our entire life to be a **channel** of divine love."[103]

We must recognize that the majority of Jesus' life and of ours is found in our families and homes, in our work and play, among our neighbors, and in our everyday surroundings. God is calling us (like with the Shema in Deuteronomy 6), to make our waking and sleeping, working, etc. to flow out of a divine wellspring rooted **in His presence** (emphasis mine).[104]

What did you glean from Foster's message?

How can you practice coram Deo in the middle of your workday world?

Devotional Scripture

Before we dive into the application and life-challenge sections, let's slow down for a moment, clear our heads, and focus on one Bible passage as a devotional. This will prepare our heart for accepting God's message to us. Consider this passage:

⁶So then, just as you received Christ Jesus as Lord, continue to live your lives in him, ⁷rooted and built up in him, strengthened in the faith as you were taught, and overflowing with thankfulness.

⁸See to it that no one takes you captive through hollow and deceptive philosophy, which depends on human tradition and the elemental spiritual forces of this world rather than on Christ (Colossians 2:6-8).

This passage captures two significant thoughts from this chapter:

- Live your life **in Him**. This is so important and is the point of coram Deo.

- Live your life overflowing with thankfulness.

We have so much to be thankful for, blessings that are irrespective of our circumstances because they are gifts from Christ where our faith must be rooted.

Application/Implication

Brother Lawrence said that he learned he could live in the presence of God "doing [his] common business without any view of pleasing men and purely for the love of God."[105] He advised that we:

> "think often on God, by day, by night, in your business, and even in your diversions. He is always near you ... live and die with Him, this is the glorious employment of a Christian; in a word, **this is our profession** ... we must learn it" (emphasis mine).[106]

John Ortberg, in *God Is Closer than You Think*, gives some practical advice for living coram Deo every day. He recommends we conduct an experiment: Live "a day with Jesus." Using Ortberg's advice as a framework and borrowing from a few other sources, here is a practical application of practicing His presence in our present:

Start: Living a day with Jesus actually starts the night before. In the creation account, "there was evening and morning." In ancient Jewish culture, the Sabbath (and every day) begins at sundown. "Take a few moments to review your day with God. Confess any sin that comes to mind, and ask forgiveness. Where you were blessed today, take time to savor it and say thanks. Give God the last word of the day."[107] The idea is that you go to bed with a prayer on your heart.

Waking: Some people can wake up early and have an extended quiet time with God. If so, that is great for you. If not, don't beat yourself up. But you should take at least five minutes to start your workday with a simple prayer from your heart to "acknowledge your dependence on God .... Tell God about your concerns for the day.... Renew your invitation for God to spend the day with you."[108]

Jesus is an example for us in this simple discipline: *"Very early in the morning, while it was still dark, Jesus got up, left the house and went off to a solitary place, where He prayed"* (Mark 1:35).

Getting Ready. Include God in everything, even the mundane chores of getting ready for work or school. As you wash up, pray, "God, just as this soap and water are cleaning my body, may Your Word and Your [Holy] Spirit cleanse my mind and heart [as I find ways to glorify You today]."[109]

Eating: Simply make this a time of gratitude. We are so blessed to have our needs met by God. *"Every good and* *perfect gift is from above, coming down from the Father of the heavenly lights, who does not change like shifting shadows"* (James 1:17).

Expectancy: "Start the day seeking God's presence and search for Him all through the day and revel in the gracious encounters of God throughout the day."[110] Realize that God is all-powerful and think to yourself, "My encounter with God today may be of such a nature as to alter the entire course of my life."[111]

Working: "Work ... it is perhaps the single most important activity to learn to do together with Jesus."[112] Include God in everything you do. Take breaks every so often and say a brief prayer.

Struggle: At some point in your day, you will likely struggle. Perhaps you will make mistakes or difficult circumstances will arise. During those times, you may be tempted to think negative thoughts. We should follow the advice of the Apostle Paul to *"take captive every thought to make it obedient to Christ"* (II Corinthians 10:5). Turn your thoughts toward Jesus and focus on what is excellent, noble, and praiseworthy (Philippians 4:8).

Rest: At the end of your workday, in the evening, remember Jesus' words: *"Come to Me, all you who are weary and burdened, and I will give you rest"* (Matthew 11:28). To this verse, "there is no fine print ... no hidden language .... [You have] God's unending affection.... You can rest now."[113] And tomorrow, you can do it all over again. Give the day to God.

So whether you eat or drink or whatever you do, do it all for the glory of God (I Corinthians 10:31).

Life-Change Challenge

Our challenge this time is simply to live a day with Jesus as described above. Pick an ordinary day; don't do anything extraordinary unless you feel compelled. Just live a typical day with Jesus, doing the preparation the day before, dwelling in His presence, and practicing the discipline of coram Deo all day. Make this the start of a holy habit.

This is something I try to do every day. It is such a blessing. When you live every day with Jesus and make every day a coram Deo day, living in His presence, it really does make a huge difference. It puts everything in the right perspective and allows us to be led by the Lord rather than feeling like a lone ranger.

Looking Forward

Our next chapter is our final chapter: Carpe Diem and coram Deo. It speaks to the fact that life is short. The Scriptures indicate that our earthly lives are just a vapor or a mist. We need to acquire a sense of urgency about doing the will of our Father.

Chapter 11: Carpe Diem and coram Deo

Introduction

In the 2010 film, *Book of Eli*, we find ourselves in a violent post-apocalyptic society reminiscent of the earlier *Road Warrior/Mad Max* movies starring Mel Gibson.

Eli, a character played by Denzel Washington, has been on a mission westward across North America for years. As the movie continues, we realize that his mission is to preserve a special book and deliver it to the west coast.

Eli finds solace in reading the book that he carries on his person. He guards it closely as he struggles to survive by hunting small animals and seeking goods in destroyed houses and vehicles so that he can trade them in villages for water and supplies. When he reaches a village ruled by the powerful mobster, Carnegie, the man witnesses Eli's impressive fighting skills.

Carnegie offers Eli a place within his gang. Eli refuses. Carnegie sends a young woman, Solara (Mila Kunis from "That 70's Show"), to at least convince Eli to spend the night by sleeping with him. However, Eli proves to be the better man when he gently declines her advances. Solara has never met a man like Eli before.

The next day when Eli leaves, Solara follows him. Carnegie sends his gang into the wasteland to take the book from Eli and retrieve Solara. But the man proves to be a formidable foe as he makes it clear that he is willing to lay down his life to protect the book.

In the final scene, Eli is reflecting on his life, his mission, and his purpose. He's made it to the west coast alive. As for the book, he knows its content so well he is able to recite it. This scene is the one that serves as a fitting introduction to our last chapter in this study on the discipline of coram Deo.

> "Dear Lord, thank You for giving me the strength and the conviction to complete the task You entrusted to me. Thank You for guiding me straight and true through the many obstacles in my path and for keeping me resolute when all around seemed lost. Thank You for Your protection and for Your many signs along the way. Thank You for any good that I may have done. I'm so sorry about the bad.

> "Thank You for the friend I made. Please watch over her as you watched over me.

> "Thank You for finally allowing me to rest. I'm so very tired. But I go now to my rest at peace knowing that I have done right with my time on this earth. I have fought the good fight. I have finished the race. I have kept the faith."[114]

Think back on the people you were close to in your life that have passed away. Considering those loved ones, who is a person that you would say emphatically, "That person truly fought the good fight, finished the race, kept the faith?" Thinking about them should remind us that life is short.

Bible Study

In this chapter, we wrap up our study and examine the idea that our future is uncertain and therefore we should approach our mission and purpose with **urgency**. Carpe diem is another Latin phrase and it means, "seize the day." One source said a more literal translation of *carpe diem* would be "enjoy the day" or "pluck the day [as it is ripe]."[115]

Today's youth culture has a similar concept in the phrase "YOLO" which stands for "You Only Live Once!"

The Bible speaks to the fact that **life is short** and we need to acquire a sense of **urgency** about doing the will of our Father.

> *13Now listen, you who say, "Today or tomorrow we will go to this or that city, spend a year there, carry on business and make money." 14Why, you do not even know what will happen tomorrow. What is your life? You are a mist that appears for a little while and then vanishes.*
>
> *15Instead, you ought to say, "If it is the Lord's will, we will live and do this or that." 16As it is, you boast in your arrogant schemes. All such boasting is evil. 17If anyone, then, knows the good they ought to do and doesn't do it, it is sin for them* (James 4:13-17).

This passage clearly explains that our lives are just a vapor or mist seen for a short time, and then gone. It speaks to the fact that we are not in control because we don't know what will happen tomorrow.

Every day when we wake up, we have choices to make. Potentially, we are at critical crossroads in our lives every day. Because God gives us free will, we choose to follow either God's path or our own path.

As Moses was getting old and nearing the end of his earthly mission, he tried to get the nation of Israel to realize life is short. Moses urged his people to make a conscious choice to follow God.

[15]See, I set before you today life and prosperity, death and destruction. [16]For I command you today to love the Lord your God, to walk in obedience to him, and to keep his commands, decrees and laws; then you will live and increase, and the Lord your God will bless you in the land you are entering to possess.

[17]But if your heart turns away and you are not obedient, and if you are drawn away to bow down to other gods and worship them, [18]I declare to you this day that you will certainly be destroyed. You will not live long in the land you are crossing the Jordan to enter and possess.

[19]This day I call the heavens and the earth as witnesses against you that I have set before you life and death, blessings and curses. Now choose life, so that you and your children may live [20]and that you may love the Lord your God, listen to his voice, and hold fast to him. For the Lord is your life, and he will give you many years in the land he swore to give to your fathers, Abraham, Isaac and Jacob (Deuteronomy 30:15-20).

Although there are some specific parts to this passage that apply only to Israel, the principle of choosing life with God carries throughout history to us today.

Joshua has a similar message. Joshua was not only Moses' successor; he was also Moses' understudy or disciple. As Joshua grew old, he also gave the people the same clear choice in Joshua 24:14-27.

The Apostle Paul grew reflective in the twilight years of his life as well.

[6]For I am already being poured out like a drink offering, and the time for my departure is near. [7]I have fought the good fight, I have finished the race, I have kept the faith. [8]Now

there is in store for me the crown of righteousness, which the Lord, the righteous Judge, will award to me on that day — and not only to me, but also to all who have longed for his appearing (II Timothy 4:6-8).

Likewise, Peter warned, "*The end of all things is near*" in I Peter 4:7-11 and spoke specifically of his **departure** in his second letter, II Peter 1:12-15. And John ends the book of Revelation with quoting Jesus three times saying, "*I am coming soon.*"

Brother Lawrence understood coram Deo in the context of carpe diem. He understood life is short. In his correspondence with friends and colleagues, he often used strong language to spur them to action. Lawrence laments about the weak faith he observed in most people, saying that most people miss out on God's "infinite treasure [and His strong] current of graces." He said we are typically blind and hinder or even block God's abundance in our lives.

"Let us **redeem** the lost time, for perhaps we have but little left! Death follows us close, let us be well prepared for it .... The time presses; there is no room for delay; **our souls are at stake!**" (emphasis mine).[116]

"He is nearer to us than we are aware of .... We have but little time to live .... Let us live and die with God .... [O]ffer Him your heart ... in the midst of your business, even every moment if you can."[117]

"Since by His mercy He gives us still a little time, let us begin in earnest; let us **repair** the lost time" (emphasis mine).[118]

"There is not in the world a kind of life more sweet and delightful, than that of continual conversation with God: Those only can comprehend it who practice and experience it; yet I do not advise you to do it from that motive; it is not pleasure which we ought to seek in this exercise; but let us do it from the principle of love .... Were I a preacher, I should above all other things preach the **practice of the presence** of God .... Make immediately a holy and firm resolution never more willfully to forget Him, and to spend the rest of your days **in His sacred presence**" (emphasis mine).[119]

My intent for this study was for it to be "transformational." This is a spiritual concept that the secular world of psychology and adult cognitive development has tried to figure out for decades. Thought leaders in the field of human cognitive learning call it "Transformative Learning."

The dominant theory, written by John Mezirow, says that the process of "perspective transformation" happens when the learner encounters something that he or she cannot fully process or comprehend. Mezirow called this occurrence a *disorienting dilemma*. From that point, an adult needs to process the new information through a series of steps including critical reflection and self-assessment ending with a new frame of reference and ideally a new plan of action with new behaviors and habits.[120]

It is my sincere hope and prayer that this study has been a tool for your own transformative learning and that it has expanded your understanding and consciousness of God's presence. The ideal scenario is that this study has facilitated change through the power of the Word of God and the Holy Spirit as we have taken this journey together.

The idea of transformational learning includes critical reflection, self- assessment, and change of heart. Even though that language comes from academia, the concept is biblical. For example, Psalm 1 and Psalm 77 speak about meditating on God's word and considering or reflecting on God's mighty deeds. The epistle of James advises that we should look intently into the perfect law of God and take action. The Apostle Paul speaks of renewing our minds and being transformed. We have studied the disorienting dilemmas that biblical figures like Moses encountering God through a burning bush and the Apostle Paul being blinded by meeting Jesus on the road to Damascus. Their lives were transformed. All these examples serve to appeal and urge us to be changed by God's presence.

I pray this study has changed your perspective and motivated you to experiment with the spiritual discipline of coram Deo. It was a way of life for biblical figures like Enoch and Elijah, as well as historic church leaders like Martin Luther and Brother Lawrence. Obviously, Jesus is our model, and He lived coram Deo in a perfect sense, staying in constant communication with His Father, never hiding from God or suffering from spiritual amnesia. Jesus was always seeking God, always busy about His Father's business and His mission.

The core concept of discipleship is the idea of a student or follower learning from the teacher, imitating and being transformed to be like the teacher. It is different from our modern concept of a university professor and a college student. With discipleship, the follower is completely devoted to being transformed into being like their master. Today, we may have an idea of "transformational learning" but we don't have many role models. In the ancient practice of discipleship, the student was in the presence of his master constantly and completely dedicated to the practice of discipleship.

We are only on this earth for a short time. Now is the time to live in the presence of the Master. It is our chance to show God we want to be His students. We want to be disciples of Christ. It is the time to show God that we accept His love and that we understand His purpose for our lives. The time to be obedient to the Holy Spirit is **now**. Solomon, the wisest man of his time, ends the book of Ecclesiastes saying:

Remember your Creator in the days of your youth, before the days of trouble come and the years approach when you will say, "I find no pleasure in them" (Ecclesiastes 12:1).

Similarly, the Apostle Paul urges the disciples in Colossae to *"make the most of every opportunity"* (Colossians 4:2-6).

God is calling us to Himself.

Are we listening?

Are we growing spiritually?

Are you living your life with urgency for your mission?

Are you living in the knowledge of God's presence?

Devotional Scripture

Take a couple of moments to meditate on this passage. This scripture captures one of the major tenets of coram Deo — to let His presence rule our heads, hearts, and habits, although in the verses, it is not in the same order and uses the terms: mind, heart, and life:

> *[1]Since, then, you have been raised with Christ, set your **hearts** on things above, where Christ is, seated at the right hand of God. [2]Set your **minds** on things above, not on earthly things. [3]For you died, and your **life** is now hidden with Christ in God. [4]When Christ, who is **your life**, appears, then you also will appear with him in glory* (Colossians 3:1-4, emphasis mine).

Notice this passage weaves in several important points: setting our hearts, minds, and lives on Christ **and** recognizing the urgent context of His imminent return. That fits with this chapter's message. Carpe diem! Are we ready?

Application/Implication

Obviously, we need a renewed mind and a fresh sense of urgency. We need a transformation of our thoughts to realize life is short. We need to learn the discipline of coram Deo. Maybe hearing the Holy Spirit through the words of Moses, Joshua, Peter, and Paul, and then reflecting on the current state of our own lives will bring about that disorienting dilemma that will lead to transformation.

How are you running the race?

Are you close to finishing your race?

Are you allowing yourself to be poured out?

Whom are you allowing to pour into you?

What fight are you fighting?

How will you finish the race? (How will you be remembered?)

What legacy are you leaving behind? (What will people say about you after you die?)

Life-Change Challenge

The previous life-change challenges mainly focused on you, the reader. Our challenge in this last chapter is a little different but still not complicated. How can you, as a disciple of Christ, share your faith and love with others? We know that Jesus called us to "make disciples" (Matthew 28:18-20).

And we know that Peter called us to "always be prepared to give an answer to everyone who asks you to give the reason for the hope that you have. But do this with gentleness and respect" (I Peter 3:15).

167

In this modern world full of darkness, we are surrounded every day with lost people many of whom have no hope. As Christians, how are we letting our light shine? How are we to make disciples and share our faith, hope, and love? The Apostle Peter gave us some urgent advice about this:

> *⁷The end of all things is near. Therefore be alert and of sober mind so that you may pray. ⁸Above all, love each other deeply, because love covers over a multitude of sins. ⁹Offer hospitality to one another without grumbling.*
>
> *¹⁰Each of you should use whatever gift you have received to serve others, as faithful stewards of God's grace in its various forms* (I Peter 4:7-10).

Your life-change challenge for this final chapter, in light of the fact that our time is short, is to share your faith, show your Christ-like love, and use whatever gift God has given to you. There are countless ways to do this. Be creative. Share your physical and financial blessings, show hospitality, share your life, and give your testimonies about how God has blessed you. The goal is to bring glory to God and fulfill our calling as disciple-makers.

In Summary

The spiritual discipline of coram Deo can be seen in a summary of our life-change challenges through the various chapters.

1. **God's Design:** Our first challenge was genuine, heartfelt prayer. Recognize God's design and become aware of your own inherent need to fill your **God-shaped hole** with Him and only Him. Open up a constant line of communication with God.

2. **Spiritual Hiding**: Choose to seek rather than hide. We must consider ways to remove barriers that blind us to God's presence and view everything we experience in the context of His presence.

3. **Realization & Response**: Change your perspective by pondering the fact that we are in God's presence **all the time**. Think of God "perpetually" and make coram Deo your **holy habit**.

4. **God Forsaken Times**: Brace yourself and others against the **betrayal barrier** and rethink your God-forsaken times, praying for God to help you see it as a time of growth for your faith and witness.

5. **Renewing Our Minds**: Reflect on the concept of a renewed mind and make an intentional plan to fill your mind with His Word.

6. **Transformation**: Pray to the Lord that He will reveal His presence to you through one of the spiritual pathways and become more connected to your local church.

7. **Our Mission**: Consider what your mission is and pray for God's guidance to see opportunities in your garden and to develop holy habits that will serve His kingdom.

8. **Spiritual Amnesia**: Adopt a strategy to combat spiritual amnesia using tools like spiritual memorials and accountability partners.

9. **Serving an Awesome God**: Pray for the Lord to examine your heart just as David prayed in Psalm 139 and be transparent as you ask God for a pure heart and the zeal to serve. Create a thankful list to encourage a thankful heart.

10. **His Presence in our present:** Simply "Live a day with Jesus" by giving Him everything: your thoughts, your agenda, your attitude.

11. **Carpe Diem and coram Deo:** Share your faith, hope, and love with others because life is short and our purpose is to bring glory to God as we make disciples.

Make **coram Deo** your **holy habit** starting today.

Based on all of these challenges, what steps can you take to apply this discipline to your life in a long-term way?

Finally, let the Holy Spirit through the scriptures we've read in this study **change you** so that you live your life with more focus, purpose, and **urgency**. We all have a calling, a commission from God. We will never reach perfection in this life but we must keep on pressing forward toward the prize.

Read Philippians 3:1-16. In this passage, even the Apostle Paul says he has not yet reached where he should be in his walk of faith. Paul says:

> *"But I press on to take hold of that for which Christ Jesus took hold of me .... I press on toward the goal to win the prize for which God has called me heavenward in Christ Jesus"* (Philippians 3:12-14).

This should be our worldview and our motivation as well. The writer of Hebrews calls the reader to action in chapter 10 verses 19 through 25: *"Let us draw near to God .... And let us consider how we may spur one another on toward love and good deeds."*

It is my sincere prayer this book has spurred you "toward love and good deeds." I hope the discipline of coram Deo has sparked something within you.

So what are you waiting for?

Glory to God! Live coram Deo!

End Notes

References taken from The Holy Bible:

AMP – Amplified Bible Copyright © 1954, 1958, 1962, 1964, 1965, 1987 by The Lockman Foundation.

KJV – King James Version. Public Domain.

NASB - New American Standard Bible (NASB) Copyright © 1960, 1962, 1963, 1968, 1971, 1972, 1973, 1975, 1977, 1995 by The Lockman Foundation.

NCV - New Century Version. NCV Copyright © 2005 by Thomas Nelson, Inc.

NIV - New International Version, NIV Copyright © 1973, 1978, 1984, 2011 by Biblica, Inc.

NKJV - New King James Version. Copyright © 1982 by Thomas Nelson.

NLT - New Living Translation copyright© 1996, 2004, 2007, 2013 by Tyndale House Foundation.

[1] Colson, Charles and Ellen Santilli Vaughn. *The Body: Being Light in Darkness*. Page 36. Nashville. Thomas Nelson Publishers. 1992. Print.

[2] Spangler, Ann. *Praying The Names of God.* Pages 15-17. Grand Rapids. Zondervan Publishing. 2004. Print.

[3] Unger, Dr. Merrill. *Unger's Bible Handbook*. Page 31. Chicago. Moody Press. 1984. Print.

[4] Halley, Dr. Henry H. *Halley's Bible Handbook*. Page 63. Grand Rapids. Zondervan Publishing. 1962. Print.

[5] Miller, Stephen. *The Complete Guide to the Bible*. Page 13. Uhrichsville. Barbour Publishing. 2007. Print.

[6] Pascal, Blaise. *Pensees*. Page 425. New York. E. P. Dutton and Co, Inc. 1958. Print.

[7] St. Augustine of Hippo. *The Confessions of Saint Augustine*. Translated by E. B. Pusey. Project Gutenberg. June 2002. Web. February 2015. <http://www.gutenberg.org/files/3296/3296-h/3296-h.htm>.

[8] Lewis, C.S. *Mere Christianity*. Page 136. New York. Harper Collins. 1952. Print.

[9] *Strong's Concordance*. Bible Hub Online Bible Study Suite at Biblios.com, 2004-2013. Web. 01 March 2015. <http://biblehub.com/greek/2836.htm>.

[10] Ortberg, John. *God is Closer Than You Think*. Page 40. Grand Rapids. Zondervan Publishing. 2005. Print.

[11] *Ibid*.

[12] *Ibid*.

[13] Tozer, Aiden Wilson. *The Pursuit of God*. Page 36. Las Vegas. IAP. 2009. Print.

[14] Lucado, Max. *Traveling Light*. Page 23. Dallas, TX. Word Publishing. 2001. Print.

[15] Frangipane, Francis. *Holiness, Truth and the Presence of God*. Page 31. Cedar Rapids. Arrow Publications. 2001. Print.

[16] Ortberg, John. *God is Closer Than You Think*. Page 40. Grand Rapids. Zondervan Publishing. 2005. Print.

[17] Miller, Stephen. *The Complete Guide to the Bible.* Page 13. Uhrichsville. Barbour Publishing. 2007. Print.

[18] Henry, Matthew. *Matthew Henry's Concise Commentary on the Whole Bible*. Page 7. Nashville. Thomas Nelson Publishers. 1997. Print.

[19] Hopkins, Gerald Manley. *God's Grandeur*. Edited by Robert Bridges. *Project Gutenberg*. 26 August 2007. Web. 28 February 2015. <http://www.gutenberg.org/cache/epub/22403/pg22403.txt>.

[20] Freedhoff, Yoni. "Does It Only Take 3 Weeks to Form a Habit? Rethinking the popular claim that habits form in 21 days." *U.S. News & World Report*, 30 January, 2013. Web. 28 February 2015. <http://health.usnews.com/health-news/blogs/eat-run/2013/01/30/does-it-only-take-3-weeks-to-form-a-habit>.

[21] Smith, James Bryan. *Rich Mullins: A Devotional Biography - An Arrow Pointing to Heaven*. Pages 174-175. Nashville. B & H Publishing Group. 2000. Print.

[22] Bonhoeffer, Dietrich. *Dietrich Bonhoeffer Quotes*. Good Reads. Web. 2015 February 28. <http://www.goodreads.com/author/quotes/29333.Dietrich_Bonhoeffer>.

[23] Colson, Charles and Ellen Santilli Vaughn. *The Body: Being Light in Darkness*. Page 36. Nashville. Thomas Nelson Publishers. 1992. Print.

[24] Lawrence, Brother. *Practicing the Presence of God*. Page 24. Rockville. Wildside Press. 2010. Print.

[25] *Ibid*. Page 12.

[26] *Ibid.* Page 26.

[27] Dobson, Dr. James. *When God Doesn't Make Sense.* Page 8. Wheaton. Tyndale House Publishers. 1997. Print.

[28] *Ibid.* Page 26.

[29] Lewis, C.S. *A Grief Observed.* Page 4. New York. Harper Collins. 1989. Print.

[30] Mullins, Rich. *Hard To Get.* Web. 2015 March 7. <http://www.kidbrothers.net/tjr.html#htg>.

[31] Dobson, Dr. James. *When God Doesn't Make Sense.* Page 21. Wheaton. Tyndale House Publishers. 1997. Print.

[32] *Ibid.* Page 18.

[33] National Alliance on Mental Illness. "Winston Churchill and his "Black Dog" that Helped Win World War II." Web. 01 March 2015. <http://www.nami.org/Content/NavigationMenu/Not_Alone/ Winston_Churchill.htm>.

[34] Dobson, Dr. James. *When God Doesn't Make Sense.* Page 18. Wheaton. Tyndale House Publishers. 1997. Print.

[35] *Ibid.* Page 34.

[36] Ortberg, John. *God is Closer Than You Think.* Page 152. Grand Rapids. Zondervan Publishing. 2005. Print.

[37] Frazee, Randy. *The Story: Getting To The Heart of God's Story.* Page 7. Grand Rapids. Zondervan Publishing. 2011.

[38] *Ibid.*

[39] Ortberg, John. *God is Closer Than You Think.* Page 165. Grand Rapids. Zondervan Publishing. 2005. Print.

[40] Lawrence, Brother. *Practicing the Presence of God*. Page 32. Rockville. Wildside Press. 2010. Print.

[41] *Ibid*. Page 28.

[42] Dobson, Dr. James. *When God Doesn't Make Sense*. Page 59. Wheaton. Tyndale House Publishers. 1997. Print.

[43] *Ibid*. Page 69.

[44] Lawrence, Brother. *Practicing the Presence of God*. Page 33. Rockville. Wildside Press. 2010. Print.

[45] Ortberg, John. *God is Closer Than You Think*. Page 155. Grand Rapids. Zondervan Publishing. 2005. Print.

[46] *Ibid*. Page 164.

[47] Lawrence, Brother. *Practicing the Presence of God*. Page 31. Rockville. Wildside Press. 2010. Print.

[48] *Ibid*. Page 30.

[49] Colson, Charles and Ellen Santilli Vaughn. *The Body: Being Light in Darkness*. Page 36. Nashville. Thomas Nelson Publishers. 1992. Print.

[50] *Ibid*. Page 264.

[51] "Martin Luther." *Bio*. A&E Television Networks, 2015. Web. 01 Mar. 2015. <http://www.biography.com/people/martin-luther-9389283>.

[52] "Luther at the Imperial Diet of Worms (1521)." Luther^de. KDG Wittenburg. Web. 28 February 2015. <http://www.luther.de/en/worms.html>.

[53] *Ibid*.

[54] Russell, Rev. Dr. William R. "Martin Luther's Understanding of the Conscience, 'Coram Deo' and the ELCA's Sexuality Study." 01 July 2005. Evangelical Lutheran Church in America. www.elca.org. Web. 01 March 2015. <http://www.elca.org/JLE/Articles/654>.

[55] Hughes, R. Kent. *Disciplines of a Godly Man*. Page 73. Wheaton. Crossway Books. 2001. Print.

[56] Challies, Tim. *Counterfeit Detection (Part 1)*. Challies. Web. 28 February 2015. <http://www.challies.com/articles/counterfeit-detection-part-1>.

[57] *Thayer's Greek Lexicon*. "Paradidómi" Bible Hub Online Bible Study Suite at Biblios.com, 2004-2013. Web. 01 March 2015. <http://biblehub.com/greek/3860.htm>.

[58] Ortberg, John. *God is Closer Than You Think*. Page 95. Grand Rapids. Zondervan Publishing. 2005. Print.

[59] Young, Sarah. *Jesus Calling*. Page 116. Nashville. Thomas Nelson Publishers. 2004. Print.

[60] Tozer, Aiden Wilson. *Experiencing the Presence of God: Teachings from the Book of Hebrews*. Ventura. Regal Books. 2010. Print.

[61] *Ibid*. Page 26.

[62] *Ibid*. Page 55.

[63] Lewis, Clive Staples. *C.S. Lewis: The Great Divorce (1944-1945)*. Wikiquotes. Web. 28 February 2015. <http://en.wikiquote.org/wiki/C._S._Lewis#The_Great_Divorce_.281944.E2.80.931945.29>.

[64] Lewis, Clive Staples. *C. S. Lewis Quotes*. Brainy Quote. Web. 28 February 2015. <http://www.brainyquote.com/quotes/quotes/c/cslewis146406.html>.

[65] Lawrence, Brother. *Practicing the Presence of God*. Page 17. Rockville. Wildside Press. 2010. Print.

[66] Willard, Dallas. "How is God with us? How can we know it?" Online video clip. *YouTube*. YouTube, 26 May 2011. Web. 28 February 2015. <https://www.youtube.com/watch?v=NhobThHUzcA>.

[67] *Ibid.*

[68] Tozer, Aiden Wilson. *The Pursuit of God*. Page 37. Las Vegas. IAP. 2009. Print.

[69] *Ibid.*

[70] Ortberg, John. *The Life You've Always Wanted: Spiritual Disciplines for Ordinary People*. Page 43. Grand Rapids. Zondervan Publishing. 2002. Print.

[71] Ortberg, John. *God is Closer Than You Think*. Page 121. Grand Rapids. Zondervan Publishing. 2005. Print.

[72] *Ibid.* Page 121.

[73] Ibid. Pages 119-134.

[74] Lawrence, Brother. *Practicing the Presence of God*. Page 4. Rockville. Wildside Press. 2010. Print.

[75] *Ibid.*

[76] Colson, Charles and Ellen Santilli Vaughn. *The Body: Being Light in Darkness*. Page 32. Nashville. Thomas Nelson Publishers. 1992. Print.

[77] Ortberg, John. *God is Closer Than You Think*. Pages 169-174. Grand Rapids. Zondervan Publishing. 2005. Print.

[78] *Ibid*. Page 172.

[79] *Ibid*. Page 174.

[80] *Ibid*. Page 176.

[81] *Vine's Greek Dictionary*. "Koinonos." Gospel Hall. Web. 01 March 2015. <http://gospelhall.org/bible/bible.php?search=koinonos&dict=vine&lang=greek>.

[82] Austin Precept. Commentary on II Peter 1:3-4. Web. 01 March 2015. <http://www.preceptaustin.org/2_peter_13-4.htm>.

[83] Strite, Jeff. *Tending Your Garden*. Sermon Central. 28 February 2015. Web. <http://www.sermoncentral.com/sermons/tending-your-garden-jeff-strite-sermon-on-finding-fulfillment-163923.asp>.

[84] *Ibid*.

[85] Young, Sarah. *Jesus Calling*. Page 381. Nashville. Thomas Nelson Publishers. 2004. Print.

[86] Lawrence, Brother. *Practicing the Presence of God*. Page 26. Rockville. Wildside Press. 2010. Print.

[87] Tozer, Aiden Wilson. *Experiencing the Presence of God: Teachings from the Book of Hebrews*. Page 20. Ventura. Regal Books. 2010. Print.

[88] Tozer, Aiden Wilson. *Born After Midnight: Spiritual Renewal Comes To Those Who Want It Badly Enough*. Camp Hill. Wingspread Publishers. 2008. Print.

[89] Lucado, Max. *The Great House of God*. Page 5. Dallas. Word Publishing. 2001. Print.

[90] *Ibid*. Page 7.

[91] Clement of Rome. *The First Epistle of Clement to the Corinthians*. Translated by J.B. Lightfoot. *Early Christian Writings*. Peter Kirby. 28 February 2001. Web. 28 February 2015.

[92] *Ibid*. Page 33.

[93] Dobson, Dr. James. *When God Doesn't Make Sense*. Page 59. Wheaton. Tyndale House Publishers. 1997. Print.

[94] *A Modern Day Parable*. Web. 5 March 2015.

[95] Ortberg, John. *God is Closer Than You Think*. Page 67. Grand Rapids. Zondervan Publishing. 2005. Print.

[96] Henry, Matthew. *Matthew Henry's Concise Commentary on the Bible*. Pages 12-13. Nashville. Thomas Nelson Publishers. 1997. Print.

[97] Foster, Richard. *Streams of Living Water*. New York. Harper Collins Publishing. 1998. Print.

[98] *Ibid*. Page XV.

[99] *Ibid*. Page 237.

[100] Hopkins, Gerald Manley. *God's Grandeur*. Edited by Robert Bridges. *Project Gutenberg*. 26 August 2007. Web. 28 February 2015. <http://www.gutenberg.org/cache/epub/22403/pg22403.txt>.

[101] Foster, Richard. *Streams of Living Water*. Page 266. New York. Harper Collins Publishing. 1998. Print.

[102] *Ibid*. Page 267.

[103] *Ibid.* Page 270.

[104] *Ibid.* Pages 237-272.

[105] Lawrence, Brother. *Practicing the Presence of God.* Page 11. Rockville. Wildside Press. 2010. Print.

[106] *Ibid.* Page 27.

[107] Ortberg, John. *God is Closer Than You Think.* Page 74. Grand Rapids. Zondervan Publishing. 2005. Print.

[108] *Ibid.* Page 75.

[109] *Ibid.* Page 76.

[110] Tozer, Aiden Wilson. *Experiencing the Presence of God: Teachings from the Book of Hebrews.* Page 211. Ventura. Regal Books. 2010. Print.

[111] *Ibid.*

[112] Ortberg, John. *God is Closer Than You Think.* Page 77. Grand Rapids. Zondervan Publishing. 2005. Print.

[113] Lucado, Max. *Grace.* Page 49. Nashville. Thomas Nelson Publishers. 2012. Print.

[114] Alcon Entertainment and Silver Pictures (Producers) and Hughes, Albert and Allen (Directors). 2010. *The Book of Eli* [motion picture]. United States: Warner Brothers.

[115] Martin, Gary. *Carpe Diem.* The Phrase Finder. 3 March 2015. Web. <http://www.phrases.org.uk/meanings/carpe-diem.html>.

[116] Lawrence, Brother. *Practicing the Presence of God.* Pages 20-21. Rockville. Wildside Press. 2010. Print.

[117] *Ibid.* Page 24.

[118] *Ibid.* Page 26.

[119] *Ibid.* Page 22.

[120] Turner, April. *John Mezirow's Transformational Learning Theory.* April Turner. *Walden University.* 22 May 2014. Web. 3 March 2015. <http://www.slideshare.net/aturner1975/john-mezirows-transformational-learning-theory-a-quick-look-at-his-theory>.

About the Author

Andy Daugherty is a full-time IT Project Manager. He has a bachelor's degree in Computer Science and a master's degree in Education. But his real passion is Christian ministry; teaching and serving in the local church. He grew up in church and over the years he has served as a teacher, deacon, elder and now a minister. Currently, Andy is bi-vocational. He is still working fulltime in IT and serving part-time at McDonough Christian church as Community Groups Minister, organizing groups, supporting and coaching group leaders and encouraging discipleship.

Andy lives with his wife, Terri, of twenty-eight years in a suburb of Atlanta, Georgia. They have two grown children, Amy and Matthew.

Contact information (e.g. to arrange a guest speaking event with Andy):

www.SpeakTruth415.org

Appendix – Small Group Discussion Questions

This appendix can assist small group leaders and Sunday school teachers in facilitating group discussions. For each chapter, there is an icebreaker question, a few questions regarding the chapter content, and a few questions regarding personal application.

Chapter 1 - God's Design

1. (Icebreaker) Have you ever experienced a "square-peg-in-a-round-hole" situation? Maybe a relationship that was very difficult because it wasn't a good fit. Or you really wanted something but couldn't find that thing that satisfied you. Encourage each person to share their thoughts with the group.

2. In what way did God create man to be special?

3. How would you describe the relationship that God had with Adam and Eve?

4. What nuggets of wisdom do you take away from Solomon's statement that we read from Ecclesiastes 3?

5. How would you express the concept that every person has a God-shaped hole that only God can fill?

6. Discuss the statement (agree or disagree): "As Christians, we are destined to have a restored face-to-face relationship with God"

7. Reflecting on the main points of the chapter (God's special design for man, God's unique relationship with man and our inherent need for God in our lives), does your lifestyle reflect that reality? Are you living a life worthy of this high calling?

8. What do you think is God's great desire for us? What is His design for you? What can you do right now to respond to His calling for you?

9. How can you adopt the idea of the discipline of "coram Deo" in your life?

10. How are you going to live differently?

Chapter 2 – Spiritual Hiding

1. (Icebreaker) Can you think of a time when you were younger and you tried to hide your mischief? Maybe you covered up something that you broke or a lie you told. Share a brief example with the group.

2. How were Adam and Eve guilty of "spiritual hiding."

3. Why did Jonah run from God's mission for him?

4. What are the consequences of spiritual hiding or running from God?

5. Respond to the statement (agree/disagree/explain): "No matter how small, every choice to sin .... WILL diminish our ability to experience God's presence."

6. What separates you from God's presence? What barriers have you erected that stand between you and His presence?

7. How can you be content in His will for your life? Are you accepting His calling to serve and give even when it isn't convenient (Jonah's calling was NOT a walk thru a rose garden)

8. In what ways should we draw near to God rather than hiding from Him? (Don't stop by just giving the Sunday school answer of "praying and reading your Bible more"; dig deeper and be more specific.)

9. How can you adopt the idea of the discipline of "coram Deo" in your life?

10. How are you going to live differently?

Chapter 3 – Realization & Response

1. (Icebreaker) Have you ever been talking and said something you regretted because you didn't realize the presence of someone else? Share a brief story about your life experience

2. How would you characterize Jacob's reaction to the realization of God's presence?

3. What was the state of Samuel's heart when he heard God calling?

4. How would you describe or retell the account of Isaiah when he encountered the Lord in his vision

5. Describe Peter's response when he realized he was in the presence of deity. Why did he react to Jesus as he did when He performed the miracle of a great catch of fish?

6. Based on these stories of reacting to God's presence, which one do you relate to most? How are we like Jacob? Samuel? Peter? Isaiah?

7. What do you think the Holy Spirit wants us to learn from each story?

8. What will it take for you to come to the realization that you are in the presence of God all the time?

9. How can you adopt the idea of the discipline of "coram Deo" in your life?

10. What is the message here? How should we live differently?

Chapter 4 – "God-forsaken" Times

1. (Icebreaker) Have you ever experienced a time in your life where things were going badly for you and you felt that God was not protecting you or even listening to your prayers? Would you be willing to share a struggle briefly (in 2 or 3 minutes)? **Leader note**: Use caution with this icebreaker question because this may turn into a long drawn-out time of sharing which may or may not be appropriate in some circumstances. With a small group, it may be appropriate, but with groups of over 20, it may best be an opportunity for two or three to meet privately with a person.)

2. If the Scriptures say that Jesus came that we may experience life in abundance, then why do we sometimes experience times where we feel abandoned?

3. How would you describe Job's situation? How did he get through it?

4. Why is it dangerous for preachers or ministers to teach that becoming a Christian will solve all your problems?

5. What did Jesus teach about troubles in this life?

6. What are some steps we can take to brace ourselves from the betrayal barrier?

7. How can someone heal from past disappointments with God?

8. If someone came to you who was struggling through a desert time in their life, how would you help them get through it?

9. What have you learned about coram Deo from this lesson?

10. Based on the content of chapter 4, how are you going to live differently? What message do you think the Holy Spirit has for you about God-forsaken times?

Chapter 5 – Renewing Our Minds

1. (Icebreaker) Have you ever done something and then had a guilty conscience, so much so that you had to do something to clear your conscience? (If so, could you share a brief story about your life experience?)

2. What did Martin Luther think about conscience? How would you paraphrase Luther's point about our conscience?

3. What are some dominant thoughts or beliefs in today's society that are counterfeit?

4. What does the passage in James 4 say about friendship with the world?

5. When you read the passage in II Corinthians 10 where Paul says we must take every thought captive, what does that mean to you?

6. Read 2 Timothy 3:16-17 again. What resonates with you about this passage? Do you believe it, or do you discount some difficult Bible passages or verses that are not politically correct?

7. What does it mean to have the mind of Christ? Do you know someone who has a renewed mind or has the mind of Christ as the Apostle Paul spoke about? Can you describe what is different about them?

8. What can we learn from this chapter on renewing our minds?

9. Specifically, how do you plan to grow in the knowledge of Christ this week? This year?

10. Is there at least one habit or action you can begin doing today to promote renewing your mind that will make it a place where you can come into the presence of God in the sense of coram Deo? Explain.

Chapter 6 – Transformation

1. (Icebreaker) Do you know someone personally who has been through a radical transformation? (If so, could you share a brief story about them?)

2. What is your favorite redemption story from fiction?

3. Would someone looking into your life recognize that you were a Christ-follower? What would they see that is related to being a disciple of Christ?

4. Read James 1:19-27. In your own words, what advice does this passage give to a Christian?

5. Consider how different Moses is from his first encounter with God at the burning bush to the passage we read in Exodus 33. Describe the differences. What specifically accounts for the radical change?

6. How would you describe or paraphrase the difference between God simply being omnipresent and the personal manifestation of His presence that Dallas Willard described?

7. How can a person be truly transformed? Who does the work?

8. Explain the concept of spiritual pathways in your own words. Which two resonated with you and why?

9. Personal reflection: Do people take note of you and see that you have changed or been transformed? Do they notice that you are different? Do you see others that have been transformed?

10. How are you going to live differently as a result of your understanding of spiritual transformation and coram Deo?

Chapter 7 – Our Mission

1. (Icebreaker) Have you ever known someone who decided at a very young age exactly what they wanted to do and

followed through on his childhood vision for his vocation? How was he different from most of us?

2. In reference to the devotional scripture, II Peter 1:3-4, what message do you get from those verses? How does it speak to you? What is significant in that passage?

3. Do you think God cares about the small details of life? Why or why not?

4. Thinking about the various parables and word pictures Jesus used during His ministry, which is the one that speaks to you?

5. Respond to the message from Jeff Strite which makes the case that just as God put Adam and Eve in the Garden of Eden and gave them a mission, He puts us in a specific "garden" when we are born into our environment. How would you describe your garden?

6. Retell Ortberg's analogy of the hedge in the backyard in your own words. What is the significance of this analogy, and how can it be helpful?

7. Personal Reflection: Using the three-stage spiritual maturity model Love > Imitate > Duplicate, where do you think you are? In other words, which of those three stages, as described in the chapter, describes your current state?

8. Based on your answer to where you are in the spiritual maturity model above, how do you think you can become more mature? If you believe you are already in the duplicate stage, what plans do you have to help someone else understand what making disciples is all about?

9. Personal reflection: What is your mission? What purpose or ministry do you think God is calling you to?

10. What new habits do you think the Holy Spirit is calling you to learn? How will you live differently?

Chapter 8 – Spiritual Amnesia

1. (Icebreaker) Have you ever forgotten something really important? Maybe you would like to share a humorous story of a memory lapse.

2. How would you describe spiritual amnesia?

3. If the Bible says that David was a man after God's own heart, then how do you make sense of the way David behaved in the affair with Bathsheba?

4. Based on the stories of King Saul and King David, what lessons can we learn from their spiritual amnesia and mistakes? How can we protect ourselves from making the same mistakes?

5. Read I Samuel 23:15-18. Why was David discouraged? How did David overcome this dark time in his life?

6. Read these Scriptures: I Corinthians 10:12; Galatians 1:6-9; Revelation3:14-22. Focus on the wording and identify the specific phrases that indicate that the original hearers of these letters were in trouble.

7. What do you think is the root cause(s) of their problems?

8. Based on the passage we read in Joshua, what is the purpose of the stone memorial that God instructed them to build?

9. Explain the concept of spiritual memorials and personal accountability. How can these two methods help you in your walk?

10. Application: How will you live differently based on this study of spiritual amnesia? What new holy habits are you going to practice?

Chapter 9 – Serving an Awesome God

1. (Icebreaker) Where do you go if you want solitude, e.g. a bubble bath, a walk in the park, an isolated cabin?

2. What verse or verses in Psalm 139 really resonate with you or encourage you? Do any of them challenge or concern you? Explain.

3. Considering the quotes from Clement of Rome, what attributes of God did the early church understand? What advice can we get from the quotes from this ancient book mentioned in chapter 9?

4. In what ways do we (mankind in general) still try to find ways to hide from God or to somehow doubt (through words or actions) that God is who He says He is?

5. Considering Psalm 139 and Psalm 23, what correlation, commonality, or overlaps do you see between these two passages? How do these passages make you feel? Do they encourage or inspire you?

6. What practical steps can we take today to be more like the psalmist in Psalm 139, a devoted servant of God?

7. Personal Reflection: Do your actions reflect someone who understands and truly believes that God is omniscient, omnipresent, and omnipotent?

8. Would other people observe your life and see a devoted believer who is awe-struck by their Lord? Would you describe your devotion to God as emphatically as this psalmist has done? If not, why not?

9. Why do you think God gave such specific instructions to the priests? Why would the Creator of the universe care to specify the exact wording that the priests should say in order to bless the Israelites?

10. Based on this chapter's content about serving an awesome God, what new habits do you think the Holy Spirit is calling you to learn? How will you live differently?

Chapter 10 – Walking With God

1. (Icebreaker) Have you ever really had a moment or a timeframe in your life where you became very reflective as if you were looking into your life from the outside and you really felt that you saw it for what it was? Maybe you felt overwhelmed with gladness and thankfulness (or even sorrow or regret) and you knew this was just a time in your life you would look back on and remember as if it were a home movie or a clear snapshot imprinted in your soul. Maybe you would like to share briefly.

2. The Scriptures tell us that Enoch **walked faithfully with** God. What do you think that specifically means?

3. In today's modern society, what does it look like to walk faithfully with God? Do you have to be a preacher or missionary to walk faithfully with God? What does it look like for a "regular person" to walk faithfully?

4. There is a common saying that says, "You may be the only 'Jesus' some people ever see" [or], "You may be the only

Bible someone ever reads." First, what does this really mean? Second, do you believe this is true?

5. The widow heard the words of God through Elijah in the passage we read. In what way can we be the conduit of God's words in our relationships today?

6. Read Acts 4:13 and 4:20. Personal reflection: How can we show courage in sharing our faith as the apostles did so long ago?

7. What do you think about the premise of Richard Foster's book *Streams of Living Water*? Do you believe that the schisms in the church have diluted the gospel message? Why or why not?

8. Colossians 2:6-8 warns us, "See to it that no one takes you captive through hollow and deceptive philosophy, which depends on human tradition." What do you think this is warning us about?

9. What is your reaction to the life-change challenge? Is it something you are willing to try? Have you tried it yet? Explain.

10. What new habits do you think the Holy Spirit is calling you to learn? How will you live differently based on this chapter about walking with God?

Chapter 11 – Carpe diem and coram Deo

1. (Icebreaker) Think back on the people you were close to in your life that have passed away. Considering those loved ones, who is one person that you would say emphatically, "That person truly fought the good fight, finished the race, and kept the faith"?

2. What is the message that you take away from James 4:13-17?

3. Personal reflection: Are you growing spiritually? Are you living your life with urgency for your mission? Are you living in the knowledge of God's presence?

4. Reflecting on the quotes from Brother Lawrence on the urgency of practicing the presence of God, what quote resonated with you and why?

5. With respect to the topic of transformational learning, comment on your understanding of the concepts of disorienting dilemma, critical reflection, and self-assessment.

6. Considering the passage: Colossians 3:1-4, how do we distinguish between our minds, our hearts, and our lives?

7. Personal reflection: Where are you in running the race? Are you close to finishing your race? What fight are you fighting? How will you finish the race?

8. Personal reflection: What legacy are you leaving behind? What will people say about you after you die?

9. Based on this study, what is your single most important "take-away"?

10. Have you identified some new holy habits that you want to put into practice? What is your plan to live differently? Do you want to live coram Deo? Explain.

87166881R00119

Made in the USA
Lexington, KY
20 April 2018